The New Ec  *ries*

New Economy Energy
Unleashing Knowledge for
Competitive Advantage

Sultan Kermally

JOHN WILEY & SONS, LTD
Chichester • New York • Weinheim • Brisbane • Singapore • Toronto

Other Wiley Editorial Offices

John Wiley & Sons, Inc., 605 Third Avenue,
New York, NY 10158-0012, USA

WILEY-VCH Verlag GmbH, Pappelallee 3,
D-69469 Weinheim, Germany

John Wiley & Sons Australia, Ltd, 33 Park Road, Milton,
Queensland 4064, Australia

John Wiley & Sons (Asia) Pte Ltd, 2 Clementi Loop #02-01,
Jin Xing Distripark, Singapore 129809

John Wiley & Sons (Canada) Ltd, 22 Worcester Road,
Rexdale, Ontario M9W 1L1, Canada

British Library Cataloguing in Publication Data

A catalogue record for this book is available from the British Library

ISBN 0-471-49963-3

Typeset in 11/14pt Garamond by Mayhew Typesetting, Rhayader, Powys
Printed and bound in Great Britain by Antony Rowe Ltd, Chippenham, Wiltshire
This book is printed on acid-free paper responsibly manufactured from
sustainable forestry, in which at least two trees are planted for each
one used for paper production.

CONTENTS

About the author   iv

Acknowledgements   v

Introduction   E-business energy: unleashing knowledge for competitive advantage   1

Chapter 1   Knowledge management: the main drivers   13

Chapter 2   E-business, strategy and new business models: creating value for customers and shareholders   35

Chapter 3   Strategic assets of a knowledge-driven organisation   61

Chapter 4   Knowledge management is about people   85

Chapter 5   Managing talent   109

Chapter 6   Capturing knowledge for competitive advantage   129

Chapter 7   The role of the Internet in knowledge creation, capture and transfer   151

Chapter 8   Knowledge and innovation   175

Chapter 9   The learning organisation   193

Chapter 10   Intellectual property protection: the legal dimension of knowledge management   217

Chapter 11   Knowledge management in practice   235

Chapter 12   Becoming a knowledge-driven organisation   255

Notes   273

Bibliography   275

Subject index   281

Sultan Kermally, M.A., B.Sc.(Soc.), LL.B. Ph.D., Dip. Fin. & Accts., Dip. Marketing, is a management development consultant and trainer designing and delivering courses in business strategy, business economics, marketing, managing people, performance and knowledge and personal development. He has conducted training in the UK, the Netherlands, Belgium, France, Austria, the Middle East, Hong Kong and Tajikistan.

For several years he held senior academic positions in Scotland and senior management positions with Management Centre Europe in Brussels, London Business School and The Economist Intelligence Unit, where he was Senior Vice-President of the Economist Conferences, Europe.

He has been involved in management education and development for a number of years, including distance learning management education courses. He has been tutoring with the Open University and Open University Business School since their inception. He is an associate lecturer in strategy and knowledge management for the Open University Business School MBA modules. He also teaches the organisational behaviour MBA module for the Durham University Business School and is a core tutor for FT Knowledge.

He is the author of *Total Management Thinking*, *Management Ideas* and *Managing Performance*, all published by Butterworth-Heinemann in association with the Institute of Management, *When Economics Means Business: the New Economics of the Information Age*, published by FT Pitman Publishing, and *The Management Tool Kit*, published by Hawksmere.

For consultancy and training assignments he can be contacted at 57 Southlands Road, Bromley, Kent, BR2 9QR. Tel: +44 (0)20 8313 3378, fax: +44 (0)20 8460 1536; E-mail: skermally@aol.com.

ACKNOWLEDGEMENTS

The theme of this book was suggested to me by Jeremy Kourdi, Senior Vice-President of the Economist Conferences, and John Moseley, Publishing Editor at Wiley. I am indebted to them for giving me the opportunity to write a book in the New Economy Excellence series and as a consequence prompted me to explore the world of e-business.

When I was deciding to write this book I rehearsed my views with my baby daughter Zara, who was then only 14 weeks old. Her smiles and body language indicated her approval of my views. However, all the shortcomings of this book are entirely mine.

The book contains some cases, opinions and articles. For these I would like to thank the following individuals, organisations and publishers for their direct and indirect help: Professor Thomas Davenport, Britton Manasco, Verna Lee, Elizabeth Lank, Kevin Jones, Llan Greensberg; Teleos, Open University Business School, The University of Edinburgh, The Economist Conferences, Systematica, Knowledge Inc., WIPO, Insead, PricewaterhouseCoopers, CIO.com, Bathwick Group, Kogan Page, Butterworth-Heinemann, Webmergers Inc., Jossey-Bass, McGraw-Hill; *Business Week, Fortune, The Economist, The Sunday Times, The Times, Financial Times, Harvard Business Review, TechWeb, WebBusiness Magazine, Digital Britain, Business 2.0, Performance & Innovation Unit Report,* 1999, *Human Resources, Inter@active Week, Information Week.*

The Wiley production team, especially Vivienne Wickham and Sally Lansdell for their professional approach to editing. I am particularly impressed with the way the book has been copy-edited.

My thanks and love go to my wife Laura for her faith in my ability to undertake the project and my daughter Zara for being so good and cheery as to make it possible for me to hide away in my study and work on this book; she has been an inspiration for this project. My daughter Jenny, for her philosophical outlook on life and her constant encouragement, my daughter Susan and her husband Thomas Powell for their pride in my work, my son Peter (Mwalimu) for his interest in my work, and my grandson Matthew and my two granddaughters Eve and Anna for the joy they have brought to my life.

Sultan Kermally

Dedication

This book is dedicated to my wife Laura
my children Zara, Peter, Susan and Jenny,
and my three grand children
Matthew, Anna and Eve

E-business energy: unleashing knowledge for competitive advantage

Overview

The success of e-business depends on converting 'e' into:

- *energy*: energy is required to deliver speed.
- *enthusiasm*: staff have to be enthused to share knowledge.
- *empathy*: the business has to get under the skin of its customers.
- *enterprise*: the leadership has to introduce an entrepreneurial culture.
- *evolution*: the business has to evolve into partnership networks.

Knowledge management and competitive advantage

The importance of knowledge

Economies are increasingly based on knowledge. Finding better ways of doing things has always been the main source of long-term growth. What is new is that a growing chunk of production in the modern economy is in the form of intangibles, based on the exploitation of ideas rather than material things, the so-called weightless economy. In 1900 only one-third of American workers were employed in the service sector; now more than three-quarters are. More and more goods, from Mercedes cars to Nike trainers, also have increasing amounts of knowledge embedded in them, in the form of design or customer service.[1]

Knowledge management: its impact on bottom-line results

Under increasing competitive pressures and with a strategy of gaining and maintaining competitive advantage, many organisations are focusing their attention on managing knowledge. Knowledge is beginning to be recognised as a key capability if an organisation is to compete successfully in a global environment.

> **KEY CONCEPT**
>
> Knowledge in any organisation comes in two formats: one is located in employees' heads and is known as *tacit* knowledge, and the other is presented in written (codified) format and known as *explicit* knowledge.

The benefits of knowledge management relate to the following areas:

- Meeting customers' expectations.
- Enhancing employees' competencies.
- Adding shareholder value.
- Generating innovation.

- Minimising risks.
- Bringing about business transformation.
- Reducing costs.

One of the key aspects of managing knowledge is facilitating the transfer of knowledge throughout an organisation. Knowledge in any organisation comes in two formats: one is located in employees' heads and is known as *tacit* knowledge, and the other is presented in written (codified) format and known as *explicit* knowledge. The transfer of both types of knowledge is important in enabling organisations to build their capabilities.

How is knowledge transferred?

A transfer from tacit knowledge to tacit knowledge takes place between people through conversation, dialogue and meetings. A transfer from tacit to explicit knowledge takes place through creation of documents, messages, memos and reports. A transfer from explicit to explicit knowledge takes place through creating directories or maps. Finally, a transfer from explicit to tacit knowledge takes place through documents and data. The modes of transfer and knowledge creation are examined in detail in the later chapters.

> Finding the person with the knowledge one needs and then successfully transferring it from that person to another are difficult processes. (Professor Thomas Davenport)

What are the benefits of knowledge transfer and knowledge sharing?

Transferring problem-solving skill

Employees who are involved in working on and managing projects do not have to reinvent wheels if they have access to information on how successful projects were managed before. For example, Skandia insurance reduced the start-up time for opening a corporate office in Mexico from seven years to six months.

Providing effective induction

If newcomers have access to information on how work is done and what procedures to follow for successful outcomes, they settle down in organisations very quickly and comfortably. At Xerox, for instance, knowledge is transferred into written form to provide customised education to its employees.

Knowing your customers better

Knowledge about customers, their buying behaviour and their relationship with an organisation will help consolidate and reinforce this relationship and such knowledge helps build customer loyalty. Panasonic designed the Panasonic Order System (POS) to reflect customer's subjective feelings about its products.

Innovation and successful market entry

Transferred knowledge can be used to gain quick entry to the market and to come up with innovative products very quickly. HP Consulting launched a knowledge management initiative and, among other improvements, reduced delivery time to its clients by reusing and standardising proposals and presentation materials.

Providing effective training

The 'Eureka' project at Xerox was an attempt to capture and transfer knowledge in order to support technicians in sharing 'war stories' electronically in the form of tips to teach each other how to diagnose and fix machines.

Building trust

Sharing knowledge and transferring everyone's experience help build trust in an organisation. 3M, Buckman International, Dow and Systematic are all creating a culture of trust by encouraging knowledge sharing and transfer within their organisations.

Adopting best practices

Sharing knowledge within an organisation creates pockets of best practice. Texas Instruments avoided the cost of building a $500 million wafer fabrication plant by leveraging internal best practice.

Enhancing revenue

For example, Dow Chemical increased its annual licensing revenues by $100 million by managing its intellectual assets.

Knowledge management in practice

The above sections have revealed some of the organisations that have used knowledge to enhance their business performance. There are other well-known and established companies that attribute their superior performance to knowledge management. These organisations include IBM, Sytematic, Chevron, ICL, General Electric, Ford Motor Co., Nokia, Motorola, Nike, Cisco Systems, Dell Computers, Ernst & Young, PricewaterhouseCoopers, McKinsey and KPMG Consulting.

What are the practical problems of transferring knowledge?

If sharing and transferring knowledge help organisations compete successfully, why has the practice not spread like wildfire? Many other organisations could leverage knowledge to gain and sustain competitive advantage, but they are not doing so. What are their reasons?

There are organisational, structural and many personal and interpersonal barriers to knowledge transfer. The biggest challenge lies in responding to the question: 'What's in it for me?' Most of these barriers will be explored in later chapters.

Knowledge management and e-business

Key attributes of an e-business

- Online – doing business over the Internet.
- Flexible structure.
- Responsive to customer needs.
- Visionary leadership.
- Entrepreneurial outlook.
- Global markets.
- Real-time feedback from customers.
- Speed of business – time is of the essence.
- Following a new business model.
- Talented workers.
- Every link in the value and supply chain is networked.
- Easy and quick comparison of prices.
- Operating within the context of an unstable environment.
- High capital to book value.
- Borderless organisation.
- Blurred organisational boundaries.
- Just-in-time inventories.
- Fast but short learning curve.
- No or very short experience curve.
- Networked organisation.
- Using the Internet, intranets and extranets as facilitators of business transactions.
- Use of knowledge is at the heart of the business.
- Collaborative and tolerant culture.

The beginnings of e-business lie in the origins of the Internet. Its use was at first mainly confined to government and academic circles and it was not until the Internet opened up to commercial traffic in the early 1990s that e-business hit the market.

According to Pricewaterhouse-Coopers, by 1993 over 100 countries had an online presence. Within the same year commercial users outnumbered academic users for the first time. Browsers such as Netscape and Internet Explorer began to appear providing a free service to users. With advertisers underwriting the costs for dot-coms, e-commerce became attractive business.

> **KEY CONCEPT**
>
> The Internet has opened all kind of possibilities and e-business ranges from product and channel extensions to radical and dramatic departures from traditional business models.

At present, the new economy is a relatively small part of the total economy. High-tech is roughly 30 per cent of US GDP. According to some experts, e-tailers' sales are rising and should have reached 2 per cent of all retail sales by the beginning of 2001.

> **KEY CONCEPT**
>
> In the new economy, which is dramatically eroding the old economy, the basis of strategy formulation is going to be competencies and capabilities.

The Internet has opened all kind of possibilities and e-business ranges from product and channel extensions to radical and dramatic departures from traditional business models. An e-business operates in a changing and complex environment. It needs to be agile and lean in order to respond to market needs. To do so, it has to have a unique value chain system underpinned by the dominance of intangible assets. The business has to identify and recognise these assets in order to leverage them for competitive advantage.

The e-business has to constantly reinvent itself and its focus should be the creation of relationships among employees and with customers, suppliers and other partners. The new business model of e-business is marked by the networked value chain.

The source of energy that will continue to give e-business competitive advantage is knowledge within the organisation and the way it is used and transferred to achieve cost reduction, revenue enhancement, timeliness and stretch – the key strategic objectives of the business.

The focus of attention, therefore, is on knowledge, how it is created and leveraged within the organisation. A distinction should be made between data and information and between information and knowledge, so that the organisation does not confuse itself by thinking it is a knowledge-driven organisation when in reality all it does is manage data or information.

Data is raw material or information and it has no context. Information is structured data. Knowledge is information interpreted and put within a context. Knowledge resides in people, hence people indeed are the organisation's greatest asset.

> **KEY CONCEPT**
>
> Data is raw material or information and it has no context. Information is structured data. Knowledge is information interpreted and put within a context.

With the growth of knowledge, e-businesses will be able to adapt themselves constantly, as long as systems are put in place to encourage transfer of knowledge within and outside organisations. In this respect, the Internet, intranets and extranets play a very important role in enabling the formation of relationships internally and externally and become enablers of knowledge creation and transfer.

Knowledge will enable e-businesses to achieve breakthrough successes because knowledge is an appreciating asset. The more it is used, the bigger it grows. It has a dramatic impact on the marginal cost of a product. Once knowledge is embedded in, say, a microchip or a software program, the cost of producing more is close to zero. This phenomenon of increasing returns has a favourable impact on the cost of production and consequently revenue and profitability.

Knowledge-driven companies also are valued differently. According to *Business Week*:

> The power, prestige, and money will flow to the companies with indispensable intellectual property. You can see it already. At the end of the last year, Microsoft Corp. with just 31,000 employees had a market capitalisation of $600 billion. McDonald's Corp. with 10 times as many employees had one-tenth the market cap. Or take Yahoo! Inc – a virtual place in a virtual medium, the Internet. Although far below its peak price, Yahoo trades at more than 40 times book value. (*Business Week*, 28 August 2000)

There will be many new entrants in a form of dot-coms in the new economy and there will also be a significant proportion of failures, or dot-bombers as *The Economist* calls them. Those who know the significance of formulating strategy, those who can prepare business plans, those with a fluid culture and an empowered workforce, will survive and gain and sustain competitive advantage.

This book is about understanding the source of energy (knowledge and how it is managed) for the new type of business in the new economy – the e-business. An e-business, like any other business, wants to gain and sustain competitive advantage.

> **KEY CONCEPT**
>
> Those who can prepare business plans, those with a fluid culture and an empowered workforce, will survive and gain and sustain competitive advantage.

> **KEY CONCEPT**
>
> The survival and success of an e-business will depend on knowledge.

The survival and success of an e-business will depend on knowledge – knowledge of:

- your employees and what makes them tick;
- the external environment, which is changing dramatically;
- forces driving globalisation;
- how to formulate a strategy that is appropriate for an e-business;
- configuring a new supply chain;
- enhancing and leveraging intangible assets;
- creating, capturing and transferring knowledge;
- establishing relationships with various partners – suppliers, distributors and, more importantly, customers;
- using new technology to embed knowledge and bring about innovation;
- using the Internet, intranets and extranets as effective enablers of leveraging knowledge.

Learning to learn

The organisation has to become a learning organisation in order to take advantage of knowledge, the most important intangible asset of the new economy. This will involve the organisation developing key disciplines such as the personal mastery of its employees (see Chapter 9), sharing its organisational vision, working and learning in teams, focusing on mental models and promoting systems thinking. These key disciplines will bring about a learning culture that is so essential for e-business.

An e-business requires these disciplines in order to be responsive to changes in the business environment. Such responsiveness in the age of the Internet means that it has to come up with a new business model and new

> **KEY CONCEPT**
>
> An e-business has to deal in 'bytes' as opposed to 'bits'.

value chain to respond to the challenges of customers' propositions. It has to deal with 'bytes' (information) rather than 'bits' (physical assets) and, to achieve this, knowledge creation and transfer become imperative for superior business performance.

Frequently asked questions

- Is knowledge management a fad?
- Why focus on knowledge management? What are the benefits?
- How can knowledge be measured in an organisation?
- Has knowledge management delivered the promised results?
- What does an organisation need to do to manage knowledge?
- Can e-business benefit from knowledge management?
- What is unique about e-business?
- If you have an idea and funding for that idea, why is it necessary to prepare a strategy?
- Is preparing a strategy for an e-business the same as preparing a strategy for any business?
- Knowledge sharing is necessary for any business. Why should it be imperative for an e-business?
- It is often said that an e-business has to think about new ways of doing business. Why should this be the case?
- What is the new model for e-business?
- How can an e-business retain its staff?
- What kind of leadership is required to manage an e-business?
- E-business involves conducting business on the Internet. How secure is the Internet?

CONTINUED . . . Frequently asked questions

◆ How can the Internet be adapted to use inside the organisation?

◆ What kind of organisation structure does an e-business need to have?

◆ How can an e-business protect its ideas?

◆ What does an e-business need to do to be innovative?

These and other questions are addressed in this book.

Knowledge management: the main drivers

Knowledge resides in the user and not in the collection of information. (Charles West Churchman)

Overview

Organisations want to win and sustain competitive advantage in a competitive environment that is increasingly being globalised. In addition, new businesses in the form of e-businesses are developing at an accelerated pace in the new economy.

Traditional 'bricks-and-mortar' businesses are trying to catch up and transform themselves into e-businesses, coming up with new business models and an integrated value chain to meet customers' needs and demands.

Knowledge creation and transfer will drive 'bricks-and-clicks' and 'clicks' businesses in the new economy. The Internet is playing a significant role in facilitating the use of knowledge, the main intangible asset for the new economy.

This chapter highlights:

CONTINUED . . . Overview

- the difference between information and knowledge;
- the historical hang-ups of traditional bricks-and-mortar businesses;
- the dynamism of e-business;
- the development of competitive advantage by harnessing knowledge.

Any organisation strives very hard to stay in business, whatever business it is in. For superior performance, organisations have to gain and sustain competitive advantage. A competitive advantage means that an

> **KEY CONCEPT**
> For superior performance, organisations have to gain and sustain competitive advantage.

organisation is well placed to achieve better results compared to its competitors working within the same environmental and industrial context. For this, it is imperative that organisations have a strategy that provides a sense of direction to achieve their desired goals. According to Michael Porter, 'Competitive strategy is about being different. It means deliberately choosing a different set of activities to deliver a unique mix of value.'

The importance of knowledge

Irrespective of the size of an organisation or the nature of the business – dot-com or traditional – all businesses should have a strategy. However, the new economy is characterised by intense complexity, which necessitates focusing on a specific perspective of strategy formulation, which will be examined in this chapter.

Managing knowledge is going to be the business imperative for every kind of organisation if they are to compete effectively. Managing knowledge will produce superior business performance.

Knowledge management means different things to different people. To some, knowledge is what an individual has in his or her head and it has no relevance to business world. To others, knowledge is an asset that can be used in business in order to improve performance. Increasingly, however, many organisations hold the view that attention should be paid to knowledge located within the organisation in order to compete in a fast-changing environment and more specifically in the e-world.

The importance of managing knowledge in an economy in general and in a business in particular was highlighted by Peter Drucker as far back as 1986. In his book *Frontiers of Management*, he outlined various developments in the manufacturing economy:

A second development – and in the long run it may be fully as important if not more important – is the shift from industries that are primarily labor-intensive to industries that, from the beginning, are primarily knowledge-intensive. The cost of semiconductor microchip are about 70 percent knowledge and no more than 12 percent labor. Similarly, of the manufacturing costs of prescription drugs, 'labor' represents no more than 10 or 15 percent, with knowledge – research, development, and clinical testing – representing almost 50 percent.

What is knowledge management?

Some definitions of knowledge management are given in Table 1.1.

In practice, knowledge management simply means locating, transferring and using knowledge within the

▊ **Table 1.1**: Definitions of knowledge management

Knowledge management is responsible for creating a thriving work and learning environment that fosters the continuous creation, aggregation, use and re-use of both organisational and personal knowledge in the pursuit of new business or organisational value. (Xerox Corporation)

> **KEY CONCEPT**
>
> Understanding the meaning of knowledge will enable people to restructure their mindset.

Knowledge management encompasses management strategies, methods, and technology for leveraging intellectual capital and know-how to achieve gains in human performance and competitiveness. (CAP Ventures, hhtp://www.capv.com/dss/knowledge.htm)

Knowledge for me is just a very high value form of information and has at some point originated in the mind of some 'knower'. It has a relatively high level of such value-added things as context, insight, experience and so on that has been added to it by the 'knower'. It is thus more human than most forms of information. (Prof. Thomas H. Davenport)

Knowledge management caters to the critical issues of organisational adaptation, survival and competence in face of increasingly discontinuous environmental change. Essentially, it embodies organisational processes that seek synergistic combination of data and information-processing capacity of information technologies, and the creative and innovative capacity of human beings. (Brint.com)

organisation, wherever it exists. Organisations that leverage knowledge are going to be the winners in the new economy. The more knowledge is used the more it is enhanced, so knowledge is an appreciating asset.

It is not enough to focus on knowledge as such – we need to focus on *what we do* with the knowledge.

> **KEY CONCEPT**
>
> It is the leveraging of knowledge that is going to bring about superior business performance.

Knowledge management and business cynicism

If Peter Drucker has been pointing out the importance of knowledge in the changing economic and business landscape for 35 years, how is it that many organisations have been slow in recognising the importance of knowledge in gaining and retaining competitive advantage? This is for the following reasons:

- Many organisations have jumped through various hoops in unsuccessfully adopting management techniques such as total quality management, business process re-engineering, empowerment and the like. These organisations have become very cynical about taking on board new initiatives.
- Knowledge is perceived to be philosophical in its perspective and many organisations feel that it should be left to philosophers and academics. It has no place in business.
- Some view knowledge as a fad. If you ignore it, it will go away.
- There is always a time lag in adopting new ideas, especially if they relate to 'soft' issues. Classical management ideas like Taylorism and learning theories have taken decades to become accepted.
- Even though computers were introduced in the 1940s, it took organisations a very long time to accept their importance to business.
- Even now, businesses focus on financial performance and on financial returns on physical assets. The concept of measuring return on intangible assets is less familiar.
- Some organisations believe they are managing knowledge when in effect all they are involved in is information or data management. There is a confusion in practice between management of knowledge and management of information.
- In many cases, organisations have spent millions of dollars on information technology and they have not experienced adequate financial returns.

● Managing knowledge is perceived to be appropriate only for organisations providing services.

In the last 20 years US industry has invested more than $1 trillion in technology but has realised little improvements in the efficiency and effectiveness of workers. This is because they are not managing and leveraging knowledge effectively. (John Seely Brown)

Remembering the trauma of business transformation

Organisations embarked on IT projects in order to take advantage of new management thinking such as total quality management and business process re-engineering. The latter was a fundamental rethinking and radical redesign of business processes in order to achieve 'quantum leap' improvements in business results. Michael Hammer and James Champy's book *Reengineering the Corporation* became the bestseller around the world as soon as it was published.

Business process re-engineering (BPR) meant reinventing or starting from scratch. At its heart was the notion of 'discontinuous thinking'. It did produce some significant benefits for some businesses. The focus was on processes and it advocated elimination of activities within a process that did not add value to achieving business objectives.

BPR also advocated massive expenditure on IT as the enabler of re-engineering processes. Massive investments in IT were undertaken, organisations became delayered and there were also mass redundancies. BPR was associated with human casualties and people in organisations remember it. Such historical hang-

> **KEY CONCEPT**
>
> BPR was associated with human casualties and people in organisations remember it. Such historical hang-ups are very difficult to forget when new management initiatives are being advocated.

ups are very difficult to forget when new management initiatives are being advocated.

Throughout the 1980s and 1990s, the focus was on the use of information as a basis for competitive advantage. Because the business world became very uncertain and complex, the origin of uncertainty was in factors residing outside the organisation. The more information organisations gathered on the competitive and external environment, the better they thought they would become at competing effectively. They believed that such a strategic recipe would equip them to manage uncertainty.

There was a great deal of confusion between information gathering and knowledge creation. Professor Charles West Churchman observed *three decades ago* in his book *The Design of Inquiring Systems*, 'knowledge resides in the user not in the collection of information . . . It is how the user reacts to a collection of information that matters.'

If we go back to basics, all organisations, big or small, operate within the competitive environment and the changing industrial structure. Over the past few years they have focused on using tools such as the Boston Consulting Group matrix, Porter's five forces framework and so on to gather information to assess their competitive advantage. In many ways, by using techniques such as benchmarking organis-ations, have become expert at gathering information and building information depositories. Somehow they feel that by having information at their finger tips they will assume competitive advantage. They feel that living and operating in the Information Age means putting sophisticated technologies in place to capture key information.

When organisations do not per-form well they question the merit of information management. However, many businesses are also operating

KEY CONCEPT

The new economy has been created and we are operating within the context of the e-economy.

within the context of the old economy. In an e-business environment, new ideas have to be taken on board very quickly because of the speed of change involved. The global village is being transformed into the electronic village.

If knowledge management is heading towards becoming a permanent fixture in the business landscape, it is important to understand its meaning and to distinguish it from information or data management, which organisations have been involved in for a number of years.

Why is it important for all business executives and all businesses to understand the importance of managing knowledge now? There are two main drivers to be considered: globalisation and the emergence of the new economy, the networked paradigm enabled by the e-phenomenon.

Globalisation

Globalisation has two dimensions, economic and business. In an economic sense, globalisation means economic interdependence between trading countries. Various trading blocs such as the European Union, North Atlantic Free Trade Association (NAFTA) and global institutions such as World Trade Organisation have been established to promote world trade and economic integration.

Since 1980, the rapid growth of both international trade and capital flows has enabled many large businesses and financial firms to go global in their outlook and organisation. The driving forces of globalisation are technological advances such as the convergence of computing and telecommunications, deregulation of business and financial markets, abandoning of the communist ideological outlook and the escalation of cross-border capital flows such as bank lending, international bond issues and mutual fund portfolio investments.

These trends are integrating the world economy in the flow of goods, services, capital and people. According to the *Financial Times* (6 December 1999):

The global village first conceived by Marshall McLuhan in the 1960s has become a reality for many millions more people exposed to CNN broadcasts, MTV and America On Line.

From a business perspective, since 1980 organisations have viewed the world market as consisting of Asia-Pacific, the North Americas and Europe. Changing political ideologies (there are very few communist countries left in the world) and a climate of collaboration have facilitated globalisation and, as a consequence, borderless organisations. Central Europe is increasingly becoming the manufacturing zone for European businesses. Workers in these countries are achieving quality and productivity standards on a par with their western counterparts.

That changing competitive climate is reinforcing a Darwinian phenomenon, which is that only the fittest will survive. To become the fittest, organisations of every size will have to be agile and responsive to customers' needs. The 'borderless-ness' is being reinforced by the emergence of the new economy.

> **KEY CONCEPT**
>
> Globalisation is one of the key drivers in unleashing e-business energy.

According to Kenichi Ohmae, because it is cyber based the new economy moves information, goods and services across borders, both national and corporate, with ease. Consumers control the chain of supply and demand. The Internet provides a very sophisticated degree of commercial reach.

The diffusion of innovation and convergence of technologies have played a key role in accelerating the globalisation process. Geographical and cultural distances have shrunk significantly with the advent of the Internet and the World Wide Web. This has enabled organisations substantially to widen their geographic markets as well as their supplier sources. The market place has turned into the *market space*.

The emergence of the new economy

Organisations' competitive survival used to depend primarily on their ability to continuously redefine and adapt their goals and purpose. The 'old' world of business is being transformed into the e-world of business, which is characterised by dot-com and technological companies. Some of the dot-com companies are reported to be losing millions of dollars a week and yet people are willing to invest in them in the hope of reaping benefits in the long run.

According to some experts, the first company to characterise the new economy was Microsoft Corporation. Its first consumer product laid the foundation for Microsoft Windows, which was launched in 1985. Since then Microsoft has increased its size and its revenues dramatically every year and currently enjoys the world's largest market capitalisation. Other companies in the category of the new economy include Oracle, Cisco and Dell. The first 10 companies in *Fortune*'s e-50 index are shown in Table 1.2.

The Internet-based company now represents a new business model with its own unique value chain. It is predicted that European e-commerce will surge to almost £1 trillion by 2004. Organisations are rushing to tap the potential of the Internet to expand their universe of buyers and sellers. There have been some casualties – Boo.com and Clickmango.com, to name but two – and many new business failures are yet to come. As Mark Halper, editor-in-chief of *Business 2.0*, put it: 'If you don't fall when you are learning to ski, you will never get past the nursery slopes.'

The Economist, in a recent leader article, speculated on the appearance very soon of pan-European Internet companies:

In some areas, especially in the market for business (B2B), big gains for Europe's economies should thereby be unlocked. And pan-European Internet companies will be better placed to fight off the challenge from American firms.

■ Table 1.2: *Fortune* e-50 index (as at 2 October 2000)

Company	Market capitalisation ($m)
Intel	191 865
Cisco Systems	187 390
Microsoft	124 427
Oracle	123 300
Yahoo!	94 833
America OnLine	89 234
Sun Microsystems	66 857
MCI Worldcom	60 531
Juniper Networks	57 293
Broadcom	56 294

> **KEY CONCEPT**
>
> The 'old' world of business is being transformed into the e-world of business, which is characterised by dot-com and technological companies.

Source: *Fortune*, 6 March 2000.

The stock prices of companies like Coca-Cola, McDonald's and Procter & Gamble fell more than 20 per cent in 1999 – the same companies that played a starring role in the 1990s bull market – so some of the key old-economy companies have also embarked on the high-tech/dot-com road.

The Internet forms the main focus of transformation. It changes the pattern of communication in the marketplace. It creates 'new' consumers, changes the power of individual buyers, alters the role of retail and distribution. The Internet,

> **KEY CONCEPT**
>
> The Internet-based company now represents a new business model with its own unique value chain.

together with digital technology, will change the landscape of competition and the way business is conducted.

Most consumers now consider e-mail and the Internet as necessities. People are now sending e-mail and surfing the net through their TV sets. There is evidence of value migration in that customers are becoming key partners in the production process. Businesses have to take this migration into consideration. The traditional players have fundamentally to rethink their position to compete in the new economy.

The new economy has also changed the dynamics of stock exchanges. The stock markets are experiencing one of the

Table 1.3: Forecast for e-commerce in 2002

- Reduced cost resulting from implementing e-commerce (as a share of sales): 5 to 10 per cent.
- Net gain in US economic output (assuming that the economy is at full employment): $10 billion to $20 billion.
- By 2002 businesses will exchange an estimated $327 billion in goods and services.

Source: Forester Research Inc., *Business Week*, 22 June 1998.

most volatile periods in their history, mainly due to the Internet and technology firms. According to a recent *Sunday Times* article, traditional ways of assessing the value of such companies are virtually useless because many of the high-tech companies have never made a profit. Many mainstream analysts do not understand market movements in the new economy. Many rulebooks have been ripped up.

Some dot-com companies are worth more than highly profitable old-economy companies. This phenomenon affects business executives who hold stock options and those who are involved in employee share ownership schemes.

Business Week (22 June 1998) estimated that doing business on the Internet could pump up US gross domestic product by $10 billion to $20 billion annually by 2020 (see Table 1.3).

Old dogs learning new tricks

- ◆ The chief executive of Milan-based Pirelli wants to turn the 128-year-old manufacturer into a new-economy leader. According to *Business Week* (3 April 2000), the Internet-driven overhaul of the of $6.7 billion company will migrate the core business into fibre-optic components and network gear where the company already has expertise. Pirelli has the technology to facilitate the next generation of Internet growth.

- ◆ Ford led the world into the age of mass manufacturing in the old economy. It is now entering the new economy by using the Net to unleash radically new ways of doing business. It inaugurated auto-xchange, a newly created online trading mart for Ford's 30 000 suppliers that began taking orders in February 2000.

◆ General Electric has started down the Internet path. Jack Welch believes in reinventing his business before dot-com businesses do it for him. By summer 1999, many of GE's leading business units were doing online transactions.

◆ Carly Fiorina, Hewlett-Packard's chief executive, decided to reinvent HP by injecting Internet-era strategies into the company. Like Jack Welch, she believes that established companies in the old economy are going to be the Net's big winners.

◆ Delta Airlines transformed its business by trading online and gains 10 per cent of its revenue through that medium.

◆ Wal-Mart Stores and Gap started on the e-business track, generating significant online revenues.

However, at present companies in the old and the new economy are complacent about Internet rivals. According to a survey in 2000, *Business.eu: Corporate versus web start-ups*, dot-com start-ups and old-economy companies embracing the Internet are complacent about the competitive threat posed by each other and 47 per cent of the companies surveyed said they did not see any competitive threat emerging even ten years in the future.

> **KEY CONCEPT**
>
> Those companies that are trying to catch up in e-business face daunting challenges. One of the biggest is to configure their business's value chain. Whether these companies succeed or not will depend on how they configure their value chains and how good their e-business model is. Yesterday's best practices become today's core rigidities.

Configuration of the value chain

The value chain is the activities in which organisations engage to deliver products and services. This involves the organisation's infrastructure, human resource management, technology, procurement, inbound and outbound logistics, operations, marketing and sales.

Inbound logistics, outbound logistics, marketing, sales and service constitute the organisation's *primary* activities. Procurement, technology development, human resource management and infrastructure constitute *support* activities. The focus is on the firm's activities and how value is added at each stage of the value chain.

Organisations aim to achieve optimisation of each element of the value chain. In configuring and analysing a value chain – for example inbound logistics (materials handling, inspection, just-in-time delivery), operations (assembly, testing, processes, plant operations), outbound logistics (order processes, transport), marketing and sales (product pricing, promotion, distribution) – organisations stand to gain an insight into their own abilities to satisfy customers. The value chain reflects the organisation's capabilities to deliver value to its end-customers.

E-businesses have to configure their value chains differently, but still paying attention to all nine components. Business is done on the Web but goods and services have to be delivered and customers satisfied.

> ### KEY CONCEPT
>
> Value chains generate sources of competitive advantage.

Because an e-business is constructed as networked organisations, the value chains of network partners have to be consistent with the operations of the e-business. Because of the nature of e-business, value chains must be continuously monitored and reconfigured in the light of the latest information on customer relationships.

The new business model's value chain also needs to embrace the process of creating knowledge within the organisation.

The new business model: main characteristics

- Flexible value chains.
- Prepared for fundamental and radical changes.
- An entrepreneurial mindset.
- Organisations have to practise double-loop learning and have the ability to change their mindset or mental models.
- A knowledge-based organisation with the facility to create and transfer knowledge.
- Understanding of the strategic distinction between information and knowledge.
- In the new world of e-business the critical resource is human capital. Utilisation of human capital and an innovative mindset will enable organisations to gain competitive advantage.

Knowledge versus information

Webster's dictionary defines knowledge as 'the fact or condition of knowing something with familiarity gained through experience association'. The word 'know' is defined as 'to perceive directly: have a direct cognition of'. Knowledge therefore involves cognition, which in turn incorporates perception and awareness.

According to Professor Thomas Davenport, 'We seem to drown in the ocean of data – and die of thirst for relevant information at the same time.' Put in context, data becomes information. For example, 'Sultan'

> **KEY CONCEPT**
>
> Information is the raw material of knowledge and it is related to data. Data is information *out of context.*

on its own is data. It is a meaningless point in space and time. 'Sultan is my name' becomes information because it is put in context. Information only comes alive through interpretation.

Data therefore converts into information and information interpreted becomes knowledge. When intelligence and experience are applied to information, it becomes knowledge; and when imagination is applied to knowledge, it becomes innovation.

Although data, information and knowledge are inter-related, managing data and managing information are not the same as managing knowledge.

Examples of managing information and managing knowledge

Let us assume that an organisation called Enterprise.com wants to launch a new cosmetics business online. It has recruited a consultant to search for information and this consultant has decided to use Porter's five forces to conduct research for the client. This framework focuses on rivalry among players; threat of new entrants – entry/exit barriers; substitutes; bargaining power of suppliers; and bargaining power of buyers. Information to be gathered under each category is indicated below.

Rivalry
- Existing players.
- Online players.
- Their value chains.
- Their size.
- Market share.
- Strategic stakes.
- Coverage and stretch.
- Profitability.
- Positioning.

Entry/exit barriers
- Economies of scale and scope.
- Product differentiation.
- Capital outlay.

- Access to distribution channels.
- Government policies.
- Market growth.
- Experience.
- Sunk costs.
- Brands.
- Competencies.

Substitutes

- Range of products available.
- Which offers better price/performance.
- Traditional vs e-enterprises.
- Innovation capacity.

Bargaining power of suppliers

- Number of firms supplying.
- Capabilities of suppliers.
- Capacity and utilisation.
- Value chain of suppliers.

Bargaining power of buyers

- Demand for quality.
- Playing off competitors.
- Whether products are a significant element in buyer costs.
- Number.
- Growth.
- Margins.
- Values.
- Loyalty

The consultant will prepare a report providing all the necessary information. This will be in a structured format put in the context of starting a new business online. The data that the consultant has gathered has been transformed into information that will be meaningful to the client. However, *unless the client does something with this information there will be no creation of knowledge.*

Like Boo.com the business may not succeed at first or it may make a massive loss, as lastminute.com. is alleged to have made. If the

> **KEY CONCEPT**
>
> The client has to assimilate this information, formulate an appropriate strategy for business and create an appropriate value chain. In doing so, the first stage of knowledge is created.

opportunity is taken to analyse failures, then new experience is gained based on new information that enhances the existing knowledge within the organisation.

This is a simple but important example. Many organisations seem to accumulate information while for a variety of reasons they do not know how to convert it into knowledge.

Every section/team/unit within a business can be asked (or people could be appointed to do this) to monitor the five forces constantly and create a knowledge depository that would enable the organisation to fine-tune or change its strategy.

Because in practice many executives have time pressures, decisions are based on the best information available at that time. This is known as the principle of 'satisficing'. There is no time to source information/experience within the organisation. To overcome this situation, some organisations are recruiting people whose express purpose is to undertake the task of gathering information and facilitating knowledge creation.

Large law firms, for example, now feel that in order to create added value for their clients they have to keep up to date with every development in different legal areas. To achieve this objective, some firms have created the position of professional support lawyer (PSL), while others have created the position of information lawyer. These specialists focus their attention on researching and collecting information and enable partners and senior lawyers to create knowledge that will add value for their clients. This will overcome the pressure of time on fee earners.

Becoming a knowledge-driven organisation

Some organisations are making significant efforts to become knowledge-driven organisations. Who are the most admired knowledge organisations?

The winners (top 20) of the 1999 *Most Admired Knowledge Enterprises* (MAKE) research, conducted by Teleos in association with the KNOW Network, were the following organisations:

1   Microsoft (USA).
2   BP Amoco (UK).
3   Xerox (USA).
4   Buckman Laboratories (USA).
5   Ernst & Young (USA).
6   Andersen Consulting (now Accenture) (USA).
7   PricewaterhouseCoopers (USA).
8   Hewlett-Packard (USA).
9   Intel (USA).
10 Royal Dutch/Shell (Netherlands/UK).
11 General Electric (USA).
12 IBM (USA).
13 Siemens (Germany).
14 Arthur Andersen (USA).
15 Lucent Technologies (USA).
16 Monsanto (USA).
17 Nokia (Sweden).
18 Skandia (Sweden).
19 3M (USA).
20 Johnson & Johnson (USA).

Teleos has established a framework of eight knowledge performance attributes that are visible drivers of the knowledge-based organisation. These are:

1 Success in establishing an enterprise knowledge culture.
2 Top management support for managing knowledge.
3 Ability to develop and deliver knowledge-based goods/ services.
4 Success in maximising the value of the enterprise's intellectual capital.
5 Effectiveness in creating an environment of knowledge sharing.
6 Success in establishing a culture of continuous learning.
7 Effectiveness of managing customer knowledge to increase loyalty and value.
8 Ability to manage knowledge to generate shareholder value.

The importance of customers

In attempting to analyse key dimensions and drivers of knowledge management, it is important to remember that the focus of any business is to satisfy customers' needs and meet their aspirations. Winning and retaining customers is the biggest challenge any organisation faces. A focus on managing knowledge enables organisations to build a knowledge bank about their customers. Information can be gathered to acquire information on customers and to build customer profiles that can be used for product development, brand management and effective targeting.

In the past many organisations have gathered key information on customers, but not used it by converting it into knowledge. It is important to achieve this.

The Internet and various technology software now allow any size of organisation to capture information on customers.

As Matthew Haig, author of *E-PR*, has said: 'The age of information is also the age of customer feedback. In cyberspace, the truth is always out there.'

Key messages

◆ Knowledge management is going to be the main factor that will enable organisations to gain and sustain competitive advantage.

◆ Management gurus and experts have been talking and writing about managing knowledge within the context of business for over three decades.

◆ The slow take-up has been due to the bitter experience of some organisations when adopting various management initiatives advocated by 'experts' and gurus and is also due to cynicism.

◆ Globalisation and the emergence of the new economy will put managing knowledge at the top of the business agenda.

◆ It is very important to distinguish between managing data, information and knowledge. It is management of knowledge that is going to be crucial for business success in the twenty-first century.

◆ Managing knowledge facilitates the gathering of key information on customers and the conversion of this information into knowledge about customers.

◆ The release of e-business energy will be triggered by organisations leveraging knowledge.

E-business, strategy and new business models:
creating value for customers and shareholders

CHAPTER 2

Reasonable men adapt themselves to their environment;
Unreasonable men try to adapt their environment to
themselves. Thus all progress is the result of the efforts of
unreasonable men. (George Bernard Shaw)

Overview

It is very important for any business to prepare a
strategy followed by a business plan. The quality of
strategic thinking affects business results.

E-businesses operate in a very complex and uncertain
environment, which means that they need to create
multiple futures. This is the theme of scenario planning.

This chapter examines the principles of scenario
planning. This involves different types of value chains
that lead to new business models. E-businesses also need

CONTINUED . . . Overview

to develop partnerships, which means outsourcing certain activities and operations.

Finally, the chapter highlights the importance of leveraging knowledge to create new business models, a key success factor for the development of business.

Every business needs direction. Without direction the organisation will be like a sailing boat without power or a traveller without a map. Strategy, therefore, is a pattern of activities that guide a business to arrive at a planned destination. In other words, it is the adoption of a course of action to achieve set goals. The bottom line of formulating strategy is to outperform competitors and win and sustain competitive advantage. Strategic formulation involves strategic thinking, which is the most important activity undertaken by any business.

What is strategic thinking?

Strategic thinking involves asking a series of questions:

- What business are we in?
- What are our goals?
- How do we want to achieve them?
- What is the time scale involved?

It involves applying your knowledge to the environment within which you are operating. The quality of thinking therefore depends on the way knowledge is leveraged within the organisation. Unfortunately in many

KEY CONCEPT

In the e-business the quality of strategic thinking becomes imperative.

businesses, strategic thinking merely involves the preparation of plans that then get frozen into budgets, forecasts and structures.

Formulating your strategy

According to Henry Mintzberg of McGill University, a strategy can be:

- a plan;
- a ploy;
- a pattern of behaviour;
- a position in respect to others;
- a perspective.

These are not mutually exclusive. For example, a plan can involve a ploy. A plan is related to a *deliberate strategy*, one that was planned to happen (a top-down process). *Emergent strategy* comes into existence as result of a consistent pattern of behaviour. This is a situation where either no prior plan or intention exists or the plan is modified because of changes in the external environment. In relation to an e-business, because of uncertainty and complexity, many intended strategies will be transformed into emergent strategies.

Decision making

The uncertainty and complexity of business create gaps in information. As a result, the accuracy of decision making depends on the volume and quality of information available. Earl and Hopwood have presented four types of strategic decision making according to the degree of uncertainty that exist over the objectives and the consequences of actions.

■ 1 Where there is certainty over objectives for action and certainty over the consequences of action, decision making is categorised as *computation*. In a situation such as this, all calculations are done and a specific route is followed to achieve the set objectives.

■ 2 Where there is uncertainty over objectives for action but certainty over the consequences of action, decision making involves *bargaining* among key players.

■ 3 Where there is certainty over objectives for action but uncertainty over the consequences of action, the key factor involved is *judgement*.

■ 4 Where there is uncertainty over the objectives for action and uncertainty over the consequences of action, *inspiration* comes into play.

Looking at these four situations, most e-businesses would need to employ substantial amounts of judgement and inspiration to formulate strategies.

> **KEY CONCEPT**
>
> Judgement and inspiration become the sources of decision making in the e-business.

It is also important to strive for *strategic fit*, because of accelerated changes in the environment within which e-businesses operate. This involves formulating strategy that fits external as well as internal perspectives of the business. The strategy has to be in tune with the external environment as well as the resources and capabilities within the organisation.

Generally speaking, in formulating strategies traditional 'bricks-and-mortar' businesses adopt a linear process of analysis, formulation and implementation. There is linear strategy by design, where strategy is prescribed from the top, or linear strategy by planning, where strategy is formulated by going through a set of rational planning procedures. Such an approach is not consistent with an e-business, which operates in a more dynamic environment.

Paradigm shift: creating multiple futures

E-business involves uncertainty, complexity and immediacy. Competitors are continually trying to change the rules of the game. As a result, elements of strategy must be monitored continuously and decisions taken as necessary. This means that strategy formulation, as we know it

> **KEY CONCEPT**
>
> E-business requires an interactive strategy. Interactiveness demands energy, enthusiasm, conviction and communication.

or as it is taught at MBA level, and the associated planning and budgeting processes (corporate rituals) become obsolete. A new paradigm has come into existence to deal with the emergence of the new economy.

In the area of strategy formulation, the focus of attention is on the creation of multiple futures in order to cope with complexity. The appropriate approach in terms of strategy formulation is scenario planning.

What is scenario planning?

Scenario planning helps organisations manage uncertainty and make better decisions. It deals with the creation of multiple alternative futures, representing situations that could reasonably occur.

> Using scenarios is rehearsing the future. You run through the simulated events as if you were already living them. You train yourself to recognise which drama is unfolding. That helps you avoid unpleasant surprises, and know how to act. (Peter Schwartz)[2]

Traditionally, organisations plan for one future. They create a mission, plan a structure and invest in systems based on that one future. When things change they are in shock.

This single approach to strategy and the focus on a single view of the future is referred to by some writers as the 'default scenario'.

Some dot-com companies have planned according to the default scenario and have experienced difficulties. Take the example of Clickmango. This internet-based business was started by Toby Rowland and Robert Norton, who raised £3 million in eight days, working almost 24 hours a day preparing their business plan.

Clickmango did not last long before it faced financial problems. Norton and Rowland declared that 'the world has changed'. The valuations of companies like eToys and Amazon began to fall and some e-tailers began to feel the impact of changing attitudes and a different business environment. Clickmango ceased trading in September 2000, a year after its launch.

If dot-com companies don't build multiple futures, they are not prepared to deal with uncertainty and discontinuity. There is where scenario planning comes into its own.

Beware of predictions!

The purpose of scenario planning is *not* to predict the future. Perhaps some of the predictions in Table 2.1 will be familiar.

What is a scenario?

A scenario describes a possible future business situation, but it is not a prediction. Nor is it something new that has been promoted by the emergence of the new economy. The approach has been in existence for a number of years. Royal Dutch/Shell made the tool famous by using it to anticipate the Arab oil embargo and also to anticipate and prepare for the dramatic drop in oil prices during the 1980s.

▌ **Table 2.1:** Mistaken predictions

Television won't be able to hold on to any market it captures after the first six months. People will soon get tired of staring at a plywood box every night. (Darryl F. Zanuck, head of Twentieth Century Fox, 1946)

I think there is a world market for about five computers. (Thomas Watson, IBM, 1943)

There is no reason for any individual to have a computer in the home. (Ken Olsen, Digital Equipment Corporation)

Groups with guitars are on their way out. (Decca Records, turning down the Beatles, 1962)

Everything that can be invented has been invented. (Commissioner of the US Office of Patents, 1899)

Creating scenarios embraces a process that is very interactive, intense and imaginative. It involves challenging the mental maps that shape our perceptions. People construct mental images and models that they use to understand and make sense of the world. Such images and models become their mental maps. Changing mental maps or mindsets is very difficult.

Perception is the process of making sense of our environment by selecting, organising and interpreting information from that environment. The process involves observation, screening, organisation and interpretation.

Judgement is the process by which we come to conclusions about our perceptions. Our judgement is influenced by our experience, culture and socialisation. Building scenarios involves questioning the assumptions from which some of our perceptions are formed.

Scenario planning is like reading the weather: it may rain or snow; there will be some sun and some light showers. Scenario planning requires us to assume a 'what if?' mindset, pliable enough to come up with flexible strategies to accommodate multiple futures.

> **KEY CONCEPT**
>
> The future is not what it used to be. There is a need for e-business strategists to create multiple futures.

Benefits of scenario planning

- Gets us away from 'one best strategy' thinking.
- Turns organisations from being reactive to being proactive.
- Improves an organisation's capability to become a learning organisation.
- Creates a collaborative culture.
- Promotes transfer and organisation of knowledge.
- Enables organisation to deal effectively with discontinuities.

 GETTING STARTED: What is involved in scenario planning?

There are four basic steps:

1 Consider the sociological, technological, economic and political (STEP) factors appropriate to the business and analyse their impact

Sociological factors relate to changes taking place in society. These relate to social attitudes, social values, changes in life styles, changes in demographics and so on.

> **KEY CONCEPT**
>
> More people are spending time online. The population is being wired to participate in the new economy.

In a very short period, for example, a significant proportion of population has come to accept the use of the Internet to search for information and in some cases to do business. It is estimated that there are over 300 million Internet users worldwide.

Technological factors are increasing in importance as new technologies become increasingly diffused worldwide and more and more businesses are becoming high-tech. The convergence and diffusion of technology have underpinned the existence and emergence of the new economy. The development of technology involves *direct* technology, where it is used for updating and innovation, and *enabling* technology, as is the case, for example, in Internet banking. Technological developments are taking place at breathtaking speed, particularly in the telecommunications, media and entertainment industries.

Economic factors relate to macroeconomic trends that shape the economic landscape. Key economic variables such as wealth, purchasing power, inflation, exchange rates and interest rates are all key determinants of aggregate demand. The past two decades have also witnessed the globalisation of financial markets and a new breed of venture capitalists who play a key role in financing e-businesses.

Political factors focus on privatisation and deregulation issues. Globally the political climate is changing from conflict to collaboration. Privatisation and deregulation are becoming major sources of new competition.

2   Undertake impact analysis of STEP factors

Analysis of STEP factors is the main constituent of scenario planning (see Figure 2.1).

Consider the probability of change and the consequences of changes on your business. Focus on factors that have a high probability of change and a high impact on your business.

Caution: *Too much analysis can lead to paralysis*, but ignore STEP factors at your peril.

Of course we made mistakes. The biggest was our expansion into America. But we had an awful lot of bad luck at home: two hot summers which depressed hosiery sales, combined with a series of train and tube strikes which kept so many of our shops closed one day each week over several months. And on top of that, interest rates

	High	Probability of Change	Low
High			
	Focus attention in this sector		
Impact			
Low			

Figure 2.1: Impact analysis

doubled to 15 per cent. Any one of these factors we could have coped with but not all of them together. And there was absolutely nothing we could do about any of them. I felt like a rabbit caught in headlights. (Sophie Mirman, Sock Shop)[3]

Brainstorm: in stages 1 and 2, involve key people relevant to the changes that are likely to take place in factors categorised as sociological, technological, economic and political.

3 Prioritise significant factors

Prioritise all the factors that fall within the high impact–high probability segment according to their importance and uncertainty appropriate to your business.

4 Construct three to four scenarios based on your analysis

Building scenarios involves questioning existing business assumptions, using your experience of successes as well as failure and your imagination. The information is gathered and organised to create knowledge – knowledge about alternate futures. According to Peter Schwartz, 'The test of a good scenario is not whether it portrays the future accurately but whether it enables an organisation to learn and adapt.'

According to Peter Schwartz, the basic principles of scenario building are:

- Asking the right questions.
- Suspending disbelief.
- Moving from scenarios to strategy.

Scenarios should be used to challenge existing business models and stimulate new ideas. Scenario planning creates environments whereby past experiences are

> **KEY CONCEPT**
>
> Scenario planning facilitates knowledge creation.

remembered and people get together to organise information, structure and interpret it to create knowledge.

> Today we are living through one of those exclamation points in history where the entire structure of human knowledge is once again trembling with change as old barriers fall. We are not just accumulating more 'facts' – whatever they may be. Just as we are now restructuring companies and whole economies, we are totally reorganising the production and distribution of knowledge and the symbols used to communicate it. (Alvin Toffler, *Power Shift*)

The business model of organisations in the new economy is marked by fundamental change. *Its strategy should incorporate the anticipation of surprise*. A shift has taken place from the 'economy of atoms' (physical assets) to the 'economy of bits' (information and knowledge).

Case Study: Scenario planning and AltaVista

AltaVista is an American Internet search engine company that was launched in the UK in December 1999. It promised to deliver free Internet access, but it failed to keep its promise. Andy Mitchell, then head of AltaVista in Britain, admitted that he announced the launch of the service before he had its structure in place and he gambled that changes to telecom regulations would make a 'free' service possible.

Cynics about scenario planning take note! If Mitchell had built in the scenario of BT not allowing unmetered access in its strategy, AltaVista would not have made such a mistake and he would not have been forced to resign.

From strategy to value creation

Organisations have their own distinct cultures. Corporate culture is defined as 'the way we do things over here'. It can either facilitate or hinder change, but it is one of the key organisational capabilities.

For an e-business to succeed, it needs to have a fluid culture. It needs to reinvent itself continuously. The e-business has to redefine its value chain and supply chain to make them consistent with multiple futures and

> **KEY CONCEPT**
>
> For e-business to succeed, it needs to have a fluid culture. It needs to reinvent itself continuously.

customer involvement. It has to ensure that information interfaces and information flows are flexible in order to cope with the dramatically changing business environment.

All businesses exist to create value for their customers. To do so, they have to transform inputs into outputs. The process of transformation consists of various activities embodied in the value chain (see Figure 2.2).

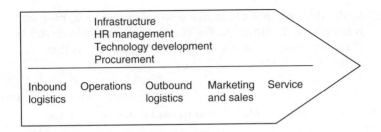

Infrastructure
HR management
Technology development
Procurement

| Inbound logistics | Operations | Outbound logistics | Marketing and sales | Service |

Figure 2.2: Value chain

As outlined in Chapter 1, Michael Porter introduced the concept of the value chain to explain how an organisation's activities add value to its products and services at various stages of production. He categorised activities into primary activities (those that directly add value) and support activities (those that indirectly add value).

The value chain of an e-business has to be configured to act as a support system for the business's customer value-creation logic. In other words, e-business has to supply goods and services that are *customised*. For example, airline customers now can book and purchase tickets online, thus bypassing distributors and retailers at the end of the chain.

In an e-business producers and customers have to work together to create value. The important factor for any e-business is to identify in which activities an organisation has the potential for advantage and to formulate a strategy that achieves the maximum leverage on these advantages.

The value chains of the organisations in the new economy affect those of their competitors and collaborators. According to Joan Magretta's interview with Michael Dell, his view is:

> **KEY CONCEPT**
>
> An e-business's value chain has to feature customers as major partners.

Boeing, for example, has 100 000 Dell PCs, and we have 30 people that live in Boeing, and if you look at the things, we're doing for them or for other customers, we don't look like a supplier, we look more like Boeing's PC department. We become intimately involved in planning their PC needs and the configuration of their network.[4]

Amazon.com poses a threat to traditional booksellers and their value chains. Old-economy organisations on the e-business track have to configure and in some cases destroy their own value chains to win competitive advantage.

An e-business has to use and leverage the Internet to integrate the value chains of its partners. It has to create a networked value chain. In order to use the Internet effectively to underpin the new form of value chain, businesses should develop congruent Internet strategies to gain competitive advantage.

Emergence of a new business model

The new business models began to come into existence more than 15 years ago and were initiated by entrepreneurs like Michael Dell. In 1984, he thought that he could create a model for his business that would involve it in selling directly to customers and building products to order. The formula became known as the direct business model and it gave Dell Computer Corporation a substantial cost advantage. According to Dell, with such a model you have direct relationship with the customer:

That creates valuable information, which, in turn allows us to leverage our relationship with suppliers and customers. Couple that information with technology and you have the infrastructure to revolutionise the fundamental business models of major companies.[5]

In creating a new business model for e-business, it is important to have appropriate strategic thinking and a relevant business plan. Many businesses act as though once you have a web site, many things will fall into place that will lead to success. If only it were that simple! In an article entitled 'Models from Mars', Marcia Vickers writes:

> In 2000, e-commerce companies tanked in the stock market, the companies couldn't get desperately needed additional financing, newspaper headlines screamed layoff after layoff, and many of the companies eventually went bust.[6]

According to a survey by Webmergers Inc., in the first seven months of 2000 out of 238 dot-com start-ups, 41 collapsed, 29 were sold in fire sales and 83 withdrew their plans for initial public offerings. Most of the failures were due to poorly thought-out business models.

Case Study: Value chain of a hypothetical e-tailer: EnterpriseGames.com

The fictitious company EnterpriseGames.com is located in the UK. It has created a network of partners by using the Internet, an intranet and an extranet.

It gets all its sales information from its 1000 branches via the company's intranet. It is also in touch with all its 2000 employees via the intranet, from which these employees can get all kinds of information on employment issues.

It is linked with distributors who supply to 1000 branches around the country using its extranet, from which these distributors can also get information on their commissions.

- *Manufacturing.* For years EnterpriseGames.com has placed orders with its contract manufacturers using electronic data interchange (EDI). It now plans to move these orders over the Internet.

CONTINUED . . . Case Study: Value chain of a hypothetical e-tailer: EnterpriseGames.com

- ■ *Purchasing.* EnterpriseGames.com used to place orders by phone and fax. Now they are placed electronically over the Internet.
- ■ *Office supplies.* Orders are sent over the extranet from EnterpriseGames.com to suppliers, who deliver directly to stores.
- ■ *Product design.* Freelance designers exchange drawings with EnterpriseGames.com over the extranet. Its staff can mark them up while talking to the designers live over the Internet.
- ■ *Partners.* EnterpriseGames.com deals with its legal advisers and accountants over the corporate extranet. This ensures privacy and security for e-mail and electronic files.
- ■ *Consumers.* EnterpriseGames.com's web site is promoted in TV ads and gets thousands of hits a day. From surveys on its site, it collects demographic data.

Re-configuration of the value chain brings about different business models, but these have to be monitored constantly and adapted to new market needs. These business models are underpinned by networks and Internet technology and these are also constantly updated.

 PAUSE FOR THOUGHT: The new business model for the e-world

'The savviest companies already are enjoying huge advantages from online business relationships. Chipmaker National

Semiconductor Corp. is saving its distributors $20 million this year by steering them to order products online, while at the same time asking them to supply detailed sales projections through the Web site. That helps National better plan its manufacturing schedules.

Boeing Co. has booked $100 million in spare parts orders from airlines in the last year through a Web site that took just seven months to build. And networking giant Cisco Systems Inc. – the shining star of business e-commerce – books $11 million in orders each day from resellers, or around $4 billion a year, on its Web site. Cisco CEO John Chambers says the company saved $363 million in technical support, marketing, and distribution costs last year by exploiting the Web. More than a third of the savings came from hiring fewer people to assist customers.' (*Business Week*, 22 June 1998, p. 72)

However, a word of caution. Don't get carried away by the new business model and forget your customers in the process. Nick Barley, vice-president of marketing for Oracle UK, says:

> This year's survey reveals many of the reasons why some companies outperform others by such a large margin.
> Not all of the top 100 regard themselves as being incredibly innovative or at the cutting edge of new technology.
> One of the lessons learnt from the rise and fall of the dotcoms is the value of some distinctly old-economy principles – such as knowing how to get your product to the customer.
> In fact today's fast growing companies are successful for reasons that have probably changed little in 50 years. Their product and services are better at finding new routes to market and keep existing customers happy. Increasingly, however, technology plays a key role in each of these factors.[7]

The value chain of an e-business: key characteristics

- Web-based procurement system.
- Sourcing – selecting and managing outsourced services.
- Products delivered directly to customers.
- Managing customer relations directly.
- Speed and skill of meeting customers' expectations.
- Managing networks of partners.

> **KEY CONCEPT**
>
> The value chain constitutes a business's DNA. It reflects its organisational capabilities.

The product life cycle in the new business model

The product life cycle concept has been in existence for a number of years. It refers to the course of a product's sales and profits over its lifetime. It involves five distinct stages: product development, product introduction, growth, maturity and decline.

Not all products follow this shape of life cycle. Some products, like fashion or fads, peak early and decline fast. Over the years, product life cycles have also been shortening due to technological development. To sustain the growth stage an organisation has to be innovative by adding more value to products and preventing competitors from copying its products. This is possible only if the organisation has distinct capabilities that cannot be imitated by its competitors.

In an e-business environment, product life cycles of breakthrough products that are first to market will become shorter and shorter. In some cases products become obsolete as soon as they are introduced, because

> **KEY CONCEPT**
>
> The product life cycle of an e-business will be in fast-forward mode.

technology enables competitors immediately to imitate or improve on them. The competitive advantage will be very short-lived. To extend product life cycles and sustain the growth stage, an organisation has to innovate constantly and stay one step ahead of the game. To do so requires the services of knowledge workers whose abilities and competencies competitors may find difficult to imitate. Recruiting and retaining knowledge workers becomes fundamental for an e-business.

The significant factor is not the shortening of the product life cycle as such but the change in business life style – the way we do business now.

The key strategic goals of an e-business are:

- timeliness;
- cost-effectiveness;
- revenue enhancement;
- reach.

> **KEY CONCEPT**
>
> For an e-business, strategy and operational efficiency become merged in the way it has to do business.

Its business model, however, merges strategy with operations. If customers are buying, say, air tickets online, they also want the facility to pay online. If they cannot do so they will move on to other companies.

Outsourcing: your place or mine?

The e-world business model most probably involves outsourcing. For 'bricks-and-mortar', 'clicks-and-mortar' or virtual organisations outsourcing is going to be one of the key strategic options.

Outsourcing involves using external organisations and specialists to undertake critical activities such as information technology, personnel administration, manufacturing and so on.

Some manufacturing organisations are selling their factories and awarding contracts to purchasers to manufacture for them. Some are using outside contractors to handle after-sales service and to design new products. Cisco, for example, has efficiently outsourced much of its manufacturing to suppliers. Food producer Sara Lee has 30 brands and it claims sales of $20 billion. Until 1997 it attributed its success to its vertical integration. However, then it announced that it would outsource its production and concentrate on enhancing its brands in order to add value to its customers. The result was a significant boost in profits.

Businesses outsource in order to do the following:

- Save costs.
- Reduce overheads.
- Obtain access to specialist services.
- Gain low-cost entry to a new market.
- Improve operational efficiency.
- Find free sources for critical services.
- Facilitate a flexible organisational structure.
- Improve quality and speed of delivery.
- Share risks.

According to some consultants, almost the entire value chain is open to the use of an outside supplier. Outsourcing should be a part of an overall strategic framework that takes into consideration organisational objectives. Outside such a framework, outsourcing will remain an *ad hoc* response to circumstances driven by cost minimisation and downsizing.

New business models conducive to outsourcing practice require special managerial capabilities. From the in-depth interviews and research conducted by Professor Michael Useem of the Wharton School, University of Pennsylvania, and Professor Joseph Harder of Darden Graduate School of Business Administration, four capabilities were identified that are required for effective outsourcing. These are:

- *Strategic thinking* – what to outsource in order to win competitive advantage.
- *Deal making* – the ability to broker deals.
- *Partnership governing* – overseeing partnership relationships.
- *Managing change.*

These capabilities are crucial for leaders of e-businesses, since such businesses rely more than others on outsourcing for their success.

 IMPLEMENTATION CHECKLIST: consider the following when outsourcing:

- Choose your outsourcing 'partner' very carefully.
- Involve all those who are likely to be affected by the process.
- Take legal advice.
- Consider the nature and duration of the contract.
- The pricing structure should produce a win–win situation.
- Develop a service-level agreement before the contract is implemented.
- Ensure that there is a way out. In a fast-changing world, an e-business needs to reconsider its business propositions on an on-going basis.

> **KEY CONCEPT**
>
> Well-executed outsourcing efforts yield reductions in costs, enhance competitive strategy and enlarge shareholder value.

Knowledge management, value chains and new business models

Competition today is not between products, it's between business models. (Gary Hamel, *Fortune*, 7 December 1999)

Companies such as Microsoft and Yahoo! have a market capitalisation way beyond companies like ICI or McDonald's. This type of company has come up with innovative business models and the associated value chains. Their source of energy has been intangible assets such as their people, information on their suppliers and customers and their capability to adapt.

> **KEY CONCEPT**
>
> The more an organisation uses knowledge to craft strategy and to come up with innovative business models, the more knowledge is gained that can be used to configure a business model to respond to technological developments and market needs.

These companies know how to generate ideas because they know how to organise and leverage knowledge. Knowledge is an appreciating asset; the more it is used the more it is enhanced.

Leveraging knowledge yields increasing returns. According to Professor Brian Arthur of the Santa Fe Institute, we are now dealing with 'cognitive industry' in which ideas are worth billions, while products themselves cost little. Management of knowledge delivers cost advantages to organisations. High-tech products – such as Microsoft Windows – are complicated to design and require huge amounts in up-front R&D costs. With Windows 95, this was $250 million for the first disk, but the second disk cost just a few cents, as do the third and subsequent disks. This is the phenomenon of increasing returns, which benefits knowledge-driven organisations.

Your customer knowledge is one of your key intangible assets

Some organisations outsource some aspects of their business activities such as the customer call centre. Call centres are used to deal with customer service. There is a great danger when outsourcing of losing an opportunity to gather information on customers and build their profiles. However, call centres themselves are recognising this danger and, according to Jo-Anne Flack:

> Call centres are shedding their 'chicken farm' reputation as staff are increasingly trained to be experts with personal, in-depth experience of the products they deal with.

In her report on call centres (*Marketing Week*, 14 September 2000), she gives examples of operators at call centres trying to understand the products they deal with. For example, 'Sainsbury's runs food fairs at which marketing services staff are invited to test products and find out how they are made. Call centre operators are invited to stores and sent on new product testing programmes.'

Organisations that do not outsource should also incorporate customer satisfaction as a key corporate objective. Various technologies exist that incorporate state-of-the-art relational databases and electronic documentation. According to Online Customer Care, Inc.: 'Advances in information technology continue to facilitate the distribution of corporate "knowledge" throughout the organisation. Customer service centres and sales channels alike can easily share information via, for example, intranets that reveal consistent, accurate, clear and complete customer contact profiles. Changes to corporate policies and procedures, promotional campaigns, product specifications, and service agreements can be updated and distributed in real time.'

Organisations now should consider investing in technologies to enable them to gather information that gives them a better understanding of customer needs. Nevertheless, remember that information is *not* knowledge unless that information is used to meet customers' expectations.

Case Study: Technology as an enabler – Autonomy

Autonomy, a technology infrastructure company, was launched in 1996 and is considered to be Europe's most successful company.

According to the Autonomy Technology White Paper, its software offers a breakthrough in managing unstructured digital information, including word processing and HTML-based files, e-mail messages and electronic newsfeeds. By applying sophisticated concept matching techniques to the problems of information access and distribution, Autonomy has created a set of products to automate the process of getting the right information to the right person at the right time. These products not only improve the efficiency of information retrieval, but enable the dynamic personalisation of digital content.

Autonomy is a success story of the new economy. Apart from having a very focused strategy, its products enable organisations to structure information and convert such information into knowledge.

AstraZeneca, an international pharmaceutical company, has installed Autonomy's Portal-in-a-Box product to manage and personalise information automatically. Using this technology, it will be able to categorise information from a wide range of internal and external sources: the Web, corporate intranets, internal documents – and deliver it to knowledge workers in real time.

Other organisations such as Clerity have developed technologies that put experts and knowledge workers from any field and industry in touch with one another.

Creating value for your customers

It has been reported that US e-bank WingSpanBank.com accepts or rejects home loan applications in 60 seconds. A single sign-on connects customers with all their accounts on a 24 hours, seven days a week basis. Employees must listen to customer calls for 90 minutes a month: top executives must read a minimum of 20 customer e-mails daily . . . There isn't the usual all-embracing unresponsive customer service department either. Wingspan has 'customer experience' units and 'customer advocacy teams' instead. Plus customers advise on products and strategy as members of an 'iBoard of Directors' – which sounds like a real e-must. (*Management Today*, October 2000)

 IMPLEMENTATION CHECKLIST: key success factors for developing an e-business

1 Deliver what you promise.

2 Make your site customer friendly.

3 Maintain trust and provide security.

4 Customise transactions on the Web.

5 Increase response time and simplify navigation.

6 Provide a value-adding service by communicating with your customers by e-mail. Give them associated information. Leverage use of the Internet.

7 Understand the need of e-customers.

8 Exploit the Internet to create relationships.

9 Constantly upgrade your technological capability.

10 Continue to monitor your value chain.

Key messages

- Strategy provides direction to an organisation, but in an e-business environment the focus should be on creating multiple futures.
- The scenario planning approach is an appropriate way of formulating business strategy.
- To deliver their strategic objectives, organisations have to focus on the value chain. The structure and configuration of their value chains make organisations distinctive.
- In e-business, the value chains of manufacturers, suppliers and distributors are inter-related. This creates a web-like configuration.
- Configuration of value chain requires distinct knowledge of customers, suppliers and distributors and also relationships with customers.
- Many organisations have configured their value chains in order to be close to customers. Customers constitute a key intangible asset.
- Configuration of the value chain results in distinct business models. The use and management of knowledge in such a model introduce the concept of increasing returns, which affect costs, profitability and customer satisfaction.
- A core competence of an e-business will be its ability to configure the value chain to accommodate the external environment and match its internal capabilities. It should aim for 'strategic fit'.
- Outsourcing is one of the key strategic options for an e-business.
- The strategic assets of a knowledge-driven company are mainly invisible assets. Customer knowledge is another key intangible strategic asset.

Strategic assets of a knowledge-driven organisation

CHAPTER 3

Making unseen business issues visible is like discovering that stars also shine in the day time. (Ned Herrmann)

Overview

This chapter examines the following:

- The key characteristics of an e-business.
- What constitutes strategic assets and how to leverage intangible assets to win competitive advantage.
- How to measure intangible assets, exploring methods of measurement such as the Balanced Scorecard, the Business Excellence Model, the Intangible Assets Monitor and the Skandia Navigator.

Finally, the chapter considers how intangible assets can be enhanced to sustain competitive advantage.

Considering your strategic assets

Assets are categorised into tangible and intangible. Tangible assets comprise bricks-and-mortar structure, machines and so on; intangible assets consist of accumulated information on suppliers, competitors, collaborators and consumers, brand name, a particular technology, knowledge and employees.

> **KEY CONCEPT**
>
> Intangible assets make an e-business unique.

Traditionally, the emphasis has been on leveraging and measuring tangible assets. 'What gets measured,' it has been said, 'gets done'. Superior organisational performance has been related mainly to financial performance. The key indicators driving such performance have been return on capital employed, asset utilisation (mainly physical assets), profit ratios, working capital and so on. From analysts' perspective measurement has been focused on price–earnings ratio, earnings per share and so on. The balance sheets of these organisations reflect historical costs, mainly those of physical assets.

With an e-business, of course financial performance matters, but the nature of the business demands that emphasis be put on intangible assets in order to win and sustain competitive advantage. In addition, book value is not an appropriate measure for an e-business. This is why the capitalisation values of such businesses are several times their book values and investors continue to be willing to invest, even though some organisations have not made any profits since they were launched.

The key intangible assets of an e-business

- Brands and reputation – consider Microsoft, Dell, Yahoo!, AOL etc.

- Organisational routines and culture, the way business is done.
- Proprietary technology, consisting of patents, copyrights and trade secrets. In a situation like this *knowledge is embedded in technology*.
- Employees with their experience and knowledge, in other words 'human capital'. Employees have a repertoire of skills and abilities. They have capabilities that enable organisations to gain competitive advantage. Their knowledge becomes one of the key intangible assets that organisations, in particular e-businesses, have to acknowledge and manage.

> **KEY CONCEPT**
>
> Capabilities of intangible assets have to be embedded in an e-business's value chain in order to gain operational efficiency.

Resources such as technology, finance and people are not productive on their own. What is important is how an organisation manages these resources in order to render it capable of achieving superior performance. In other words, the core competence of any organisation is its ability to co-ordinate and leverage its resources in order to achieve its strategic objectives. Core competence, according to strategy gurus Hamel and Prahalad, enhances the value delivered to customers.

Businesses can gain and sustain competitive advantage if their competitors fail to imitate them. For an e-business to compete successfully, it has to have a distinct capability to use its intangible assets effectively. Intangible assets and their associated competencies are the most difficult things for a competitor to imitate. The restriction of imitation is one of the key factors that enable organisations to sustain competitive advantage.

Knowledge management and the value of intangible assets

Brands

A brand is a name, sign, symbol or design or a combination of these intended to reflect and communicate the values of products, services or the organisation. A brand communicates attributes (such as speed, quality, durability), benefits (comfort, safety), values (safety, high performance), and personality (matching the desired self-image of buyers with the brand's image).

Brands such as Microsoft, Dell, IBM, Yahoo! and AOL reflect corporate values. What matters is not only the perception of customers but also that of employees. Brands don't only simplify products or services; when celebrities are used to promote certain products or services, 'personal brands' may be said to exist.

> **KEY CONCEPT**
>
> What the customer perceives, the customer must receive.

Consumers establish a set of beliefs about a particular brand. These beliefs are based on perceptions, which in turn create expectations. What the organisation has to do is manage these expectations.

A powerful brand has high brand equity to the extent that it has higher brand loyalty, name awareness and perceived quality. A brand with strong brand equity is a very valuable intangible asset. However, brand equity does not usually appear in a balance sheet because it is very difficult to measure.

It is now possible to establish brand equity in a short period. Yahoo! was founded in 1994 and has now become a household name, with 38 million users per month. It is reported to have greater visibility than many conventional media organisations such as MTV and CNBC. AOL is another example of a company that has built brand image quickly. However, brand equity incorporates service excellence.

Without service excellence, brand equity cannot be sustained. Zemke and Connellan emphasise that in marketing terms it is not price, product or place that provides differentiation – it's the quality of service.[8] Research shows that 30–80 per cent of all Web shopping carts are abandoned due to poor quality of service. Spending a very high proportion of venture capital on advertising and promotion is not enough if companies fail to provide quality service. Having an established brand is also onerous in that it is associated with service excellence in customers' perception. If you don't deliver what you promise, it will ultimately damage your business.

To use a brand as an intangible asset, an e-business has to *acquire* and *manage* knowledge about how its brand is perceived by customers, employees and partners. The Internet can be used to undertake surveys and at the same time to create relationships with various stakeholders. It is very important to build brand equity.

If a business can acquire and manage knowledge of its stakeholders effectively, it can enhance its brand and thus increase the value of its business. The Microsoft brand, for example, stands for innovation and leading-edge technology. The company's market value is enhanced as a result of this perception. However, Microsoft has to continue getting information on the perception of its brand in order to transform its information into knowledge. Without such knowledge, the brand perception will eventually weaken and the business could lose value.

Corporate culture

Corporate culture provides the context within which business decisions are made and implemented. It can be defined simply as 'the way we do business around here'. It is very

> **KEY CONCEPT**
>
> Corporate culture can either be a hindrance or a help in managing business transformation.

important for an e-business that constantly has to change to respond to market needs. Corporate culture is one of the main constituents of organisational capability.

Corporate culture involves the shared beliefs, values and expectations of people in the organisation. It influences the performance of every individual and consequently the performance of the organisation.

Corporate culture can be a hindrance or a facilitator of superior performance. Behaviour influenced by corporate culture can determine the degree of creativity and innovation in the organisation.

■ *Collaborative culture.* In such a culture the degree of sociability and solidarity of employees throughout the organisation is very high and as a consequence the performance of the organisation as a whole is effective.
■ *Co-operative culture.* In such a culture employees do co-operate, but the degree of interpersonal effectiveness is low. The lack of sociability or interpersonal closeness reduces the effectiveness of the organisation's performance.
■ *Co-existence culture.* In this culture different groups of employees (financiers, marketers, technicians) tolerate each other's existence but the degree of trust is very low. Groups try to work independently of one another.
■ *Conflict culture.* In this culture different groups of employees are constantly in conflict with one another. Organisational performance is low and market forces will soon eliminate such organisations.

How do companies leverage culture change?

Organisations introduce change initiatives either out of desperation or in an attempt to react to market forces. The key mechanisms used by organisations to bring about cultural change have been the following:

- Introducing new management initiatives, such as total quality management (TQM).
- Becoming customer focused.
- Reengineering processes.
- Empowering employees.
- Forming cross-functional teams.

The culture of an e-business has to be collaborative in order for business to be able to constantly reinvent itself. For this the culture must involve:

- tolerance;
- empowerment of employees;
- trust;
- networking;
- open communication;
- recognition;
- diversity;
- talented individuals.

> **KEY CONCEPT**
>
> The culture of an e-business can be defined as 'the way we do things in response to our customers' needs'.

Again, this list is not exhaustive but these factors are necessary if an e-business is to be agile and lean.

The importance of organisational culture

- It creates a sense of identity.
- It enhances commitment to the organisation's mission.
- It reinforces standards of behaviour.

A rigid corporate culture can stifle creativity and innovation. A collaborative culture, in contrast, embodies trust and open and free communication, which is required for creating, sharing and transferring knowledge in the organisation. Corporate culture is a key element of any business, and in particular an e-business, if knowledge is to be used to gain and sustain competitive advantage.

Technology

Use of proprietary technology, patents, copyrights, trade secrets, the way the business uses the Internet, its intranet and extranet to build its value chain and arrive at a new business model all constitute intangible assets. Such assets enable the business to create and transfer knowledge and also to build relationships with customers, suppliers and distributors.

The strength of the value chain and its effectiveness depend on how the business uses such enablers. Technology and the Internet in particular can be an enabler of superior performance, as outlined in more depth in Chapter 7. By using technology, e-business can dramatically enhance revenues and lower transaction costs within the value chain, thus enhancing its shareholder value.

At this stage, it is important to remember that technology is only an enabler. What is significant is how the intangible asset of technology is used to create and transfer knowledge, which is an essential ingredient of business transformation.

Employees

'Our people are our greatest asset.' Statements such as this have appeared in the annual reports of many companies, including those who have 'abused' their employees by discriminating against them, bullying them, sacking them and so on.

For an e-business, people *are* its greatest assets. It requires creativity, innovation and knowledge and only people within the business can provide that. Chapter 5 is devoted to managing an organisation's talent.

Measuring intangible assets

Measurement of performance is important for any business. Performance measurement is undertaken to identify:

- if the business is meeting its strategic objectives;
- if customers are being satisfied;
- if employees' aspirations and needs are met and their behaviour is congruent with business objectives;
- if shareholder value is being enhanced;
- if all stakeholders' needs taken into account in formulating the strategy are being met.

E-business shifts value from tangible to intangible assets. In order to measure the performance of the business, it becomes necessary to measure the performance of its intangible assets. This is a daunting challenge, because businesses

> **KEY CONCEPT**
>
> Making the best use of knowledge requires behaviour, technology and measurement.

tend to focus their attention on financial indicators and their balance sheets are dominated by tangible assets. Great efforts are now being made to measure intangible assets and new methods are evolving gradually. The measurement methods examined in this chapter are the Balanced Scorecard, the Intangible Assets Monitor and the Skandia Navigator.

Balanced Scorecard

The Balanced Scorecard was designed by Professor Robert Kaplan of Harvard Business School and Dr David Norton, president of Renaissance Strategy Group. It provides a comprehensive framework for translating a company's strategic objectives into a meaningful set of performance measurements. It embraces the following four perspectives (see Figure 3.1):

- *Financial perspective* – cash flow, shareholder value, profits, earnings per share and so on.

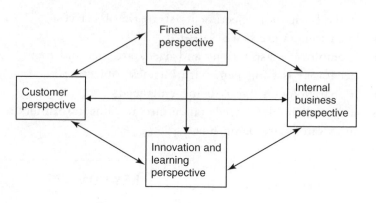

Figure 3.1: Balanced Scorecard

- *Customer perspective* – the number and categories of customers, repeat business, customer satisfaction, on-time delivery and so on.
- *Internal business perspective* – speed of fulfilment, safety, time to market and so on.
- *Innovation and learning perspective* – number and types of employees, skills portfolio, employee satisfaction, innovation, brand management and so on.

This method of measurement was introduced because, as the authors stated:

> the financial accounting model should have been expanded to incorporate the valuation of a company's intangible and intellectual assets, such as high-quality products and services, motivated and skilled employees, responsive and predictable internal processes, and satisfied and loyal customers. Such a valuation of intangible assets and company capabilities would be especially helpful since, for information age companies, these assets are more critical to success than traditional physical and tangible assets. If intangible assets and companies could be valued within the financial accounting model, organisations that enhanced

these assets and capabilities could communicate this improvement to employees, shareholders, creditors and communities.[9]

The Balanced Scorecard and e-business

An e-business's strategic goals should be revenue enhancement, cost reduction, speed, timeliness, stretch, customer satisfaction and employee involvement and creativity. These elements are incorporated in its value chain. These goals can be measured by devising appropriate performance indicators to fall within the four categories.

Under *financial perspective*, indicators such as revenue, costs, profits and earnings per share would be considered. Under *customer perspective*, one could look at customer responsiveness, customer base, customer relationship, complaints, brand perception and strength. Under *internal business perspective*, timeliness and ease of using the web site could be looked at; and under *innovation and learning perspective* consider indicators that relate to skill building, innovation, knowledge sharing and relationships with customers, colleagues and partners.

> **KEY CONCEPT**
>
> The best people to come up with appropriate indicators to measure intangible assets are the people who are doing the job – employees.

The type of scorecard approach used will depend on the nature of the organisation and the business it is in. The Balanced Scorecard is used by many companies, so it should not be difficult to make the transition to thinking of different indicators as traditional companies begin to undertake e-business.

Business Excellence Model

The Business Excellence Model (formerly known as the European Quality Foundation Model) was introduced by

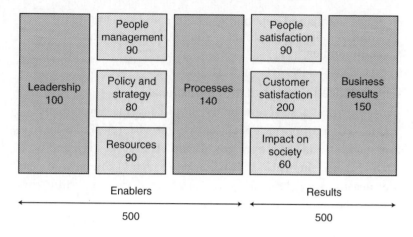

Figure 3.2: Business Excellence Model

the European Quality Foundation in order to promote the measurement of total quality. Total quality embraces all dimensions – tangible and intangible – of business.

The model is divided into *enablers* and *results* (see Figure 3.2). The enablers of business excellence are leadership, people management, policy and strategy, resources and processes. The results are people satisfaction, customer satisfaction, impact on society and business results.

◆ *Leadership* is key to any business. What is measured here is the visible involvement of the leader: the way the leadership communicates corporate value, timely recognition and appreciation of the efforts of individuals and the teams in the business, and involvement with suppliers and customers.

◆ *People management.* How the company releases the full potential of its people to improve the business continuously. Evidence is required of how human resources are planned and how the skills and capabilities of employees are planned and realised. Empowerment of

people and effective top-down and bottom-up communication are also considered.

◆ *Policy and strategy.* How the company incorporates the
concept of total quality in the determination, communication and implementation, review and improvement of
its policy and strategy.

◆ *Resources.* How the company improves its business
continuously based on the concept of total quality,
including the management of financial, information
and technological resources and of suppliers and
materials.

◆ *Processes.* How key and
support services are identified, reviewed and revised
to ensure the continuous
improvement of the
business.

> **KEY CONCEPT**
>
> Configuration of the Business
> Excellence Model can serve a
> useful purpose in measuring the
> performance of an e-business.

◆ *Customer satisfaction.* Assessing the capability to meet
product and service specifications, timely delivery,
reliability, how complaints are handled.

◆ *People satisfaction.* This category focuses on the organisation's efforts to meet its aspirations and needs in relation
to providing a good working environment and career
development, reward and recognition.

◆ *Impact on society.* The impact of organisational performance on society in general, for example the creation of
local employment.

◆ *Business results.* The results achieved according to the
organisation's strategic objectives.

This model has been in existence for over two decades.
Because most companies are conversant with it and because it
incorporates assessment and measurement of intangible
assets, it can be adopted and adapted to measure the
performance of an e-business.

Case study: Systematic

Systematic is an independent Danish software house with subsidiaries in the UK and the USA. It is a knowledge-based company with more than 150 employees of which two-thirds have a university degree in computer science, electronics, civil engineering etc.

Being a high-tech IT company, Systematic's most important resource is knowledge. The foundation of the company is based first and foremost on the knowledge and competency of its employees (human capital), but also the knowledge and experience of customers, processes and technologies (structural capital). Systematic explains:

> Our aim is the creation, development and utilisation of this knowledge . . . Core competence is delivery on time and to quality, and with the functionality, agreed with the customer . . . One third of the total group resources are engaged in the development, marketing and support of our products . . . Systematic's key assets are the knowledge, experience and commitment of our employees. The ability to attract, develop and retain the best computer scientists and systems engineers is crucial for the company's success. We must, therefore, provide interesting and challenging tasks and an inspiring working environment. The implementation of new IT systems normally has a huge impact on the way in which our customers work and on the customers' success in their business areas. It is therefore essential that we work closely together with our customers.

Systematic prepares an Intellectual Capital Report to assess its 'soft' assets:

CONTINUED . . . Case study: Systematic

The Intellectual Capital Report aims to describe all essential activities in Systematic related to knowledge. The measurements are based primarily on data from our financial accounting system, staff system and analyses conducted by external parties/consultants (satisfaction surveys and process assessments). Metrics may be abolished and replaced by more relevant ones as the company develops and new requirements arise.

The business goals of Systematic as measured by an adapted Business Excellence Model are as follows:

Financial goals

1 Increase turnover by 25 to 30 per cent annually.
2 Maintain net profit ratio (operating profit in relation to turnover) of at least 10 per cent.
3 Research and development costs of at least 10 per cent of turnover.

Customer and product goals

1 Increase customer base by two or three new strategic customers per year.
2 Increase turnover from non-defence project customers to at least half of the total project turnover by 2000/ 2001.
3 Be perceived as a world-leading supplier of products for interoperability between defence organisations, and a leading supplier of products for Electronic Data Interchange.
4 Maintain customer satisfaction at a minimum level of 4.0 on a scale of 1 to 5.

CONTINUED ... Case study: Systematic

Human resource goals

1 Maintain a high level of education among employees.
2 Enhance skills through continuous on-the-job challenges and at least five training course days per employee per year.
3 Maintain employee satisfaction at a minimum level of 3.5 on a scale from 1 to 5.

Quality and process goals

1 Be among the top quality software companies and be certified at level 3 according to the Capability Maturity Model by the year 2000.
2 Improve performance in the software development process by at least 15 per cent over three years.
3 Implement a system for efficient knowledge management by the year 2000.

The business objectives are measured under the categories of customers, employees, processes, infrastructure (supporting the business processes), innovation, external relationships and knowledge management.

By knowledge management we mean the processes and systems that contribute to build, maintain and diversify relevant knowledge to support individual employees in their everyday jobs and by developing employee and company capabilities.

Knowledge management is therefore not only a matter of knowledge databases and technology but rather of human resources and capability development.

As the company grows, we can see an increasing need for knowledge structure and knowledge sharing

---

CONTINUED . . . Case study: Systematic

across projects and departments. It is crucial for our competitiveness that each employee is able to identify existing knowledge and where to find it, quickly and effectively.

For future developments the focus is on the following tasks:

Knowledge sharing

- Prepare a list of subject matter experts.
- Strengthen our intranet by a document search system.
- Structure and qualify 'best practices'.
- Implement a system for maintaining knowledge and experience relevant to other projects.

Knowledge development

- Establish a system for the knowledge and competence aspect of annual performance reviews.
- Intensify the Software Process Improvement project (SPI), which focuses on improvement of all procedures, processes etc.

Source: Systematic's Intellectual Capital Report, 1999 and extracts from its Annual Report 1997/98.

Intangible assets monitor

This is a measurement model devised by Karl Erik Sveiby. According to him, the intangible assets on an organisation's balance sheet constitute a family of three: external structure, internal structure and employee competence.

◆ *External structure* refers to customer and supplier relationships and the organisation's image. This category of asset also includes relationships with competitors and collaborators.

◆ *Internal structure* includes patents, concepts, models and computer and administration systems that are part of the organisation. The internal structure is part of the value chain and it includes culture.

◆ *Employee competence* refers to the capacity of employees to act in a wide variety of situations. It includes their education, experience, skills, attitude and energy.

The three categories of intangible asset are inter-related. The performance indicators under each category relate to growth, efficiency and stability.

Measuring internal structure

For example, under internal structure the following indicators can be considered:

■ *Growth/renewal*: Rate of investment in new methods and systems. Investment in information technology expressed as a percentage of turnover, which can provide a valuable clue as to how the internal structure is developing.

■ *Efficiency*: Proportion of support staff to total number of employees. Sales per employee.

■ *Stability*: Staff turnover. 'Rookie ratio', the number of people with less than two years' employment.

Measuring external structure

■ *Growth/renewal*: Profitability per customer. Organic growth – how fast your business is growing.

■ *Efficiency*: Satisfied customer index, measuring the degree of customer satisfaction. Sales per customer.

■ *Stability*: Proportion of major key accounts. Age structure of customers. Repeat business.

An e-business deals more with intangible than tangible assets. Customers' and suppliers' relationships become crucial in doing business successfully and its internal structure, reflected in the value chain and incorporating the Internet, intranet

> **KEY CONCEPT**
>
> Clicks, as opposed to bricks, businesses have to pay more attention to intangible assets.

and extranet, becomes the key enabler. Employee competence creates creativity and innovation. Again, each business has to involve its employees in coming up with appropriate measurement indicators.

According to Sveiby, creating value by leveraging intangible assets is what managing knowledge is all about: 'To be able to do that, you have to visualise your organisation as consisting of nothing but knowledge and knowledge flows.' Since intangible assets are important, every opportunity should be taken by the business to enhance and leverage these assets.

Skandia Navigator

The navigator is a tool for measuring intellectual capital devised by Skandia AFS, a Swedish financial services company (see Figure 3.3). Skandia felt there was a need to highlight the value of intangible assets to the business. It decided to take stock of its intangible assets in 1992 and came up with a definition of intellectual capital, which was human capital + structural capital.

Human capital puts the focus on people. *Structural capital* is represented by such things as the customer database, IT systems etc. Human capital cannot be owned, it can only be rented, whereas structural capital can be owned and traded.

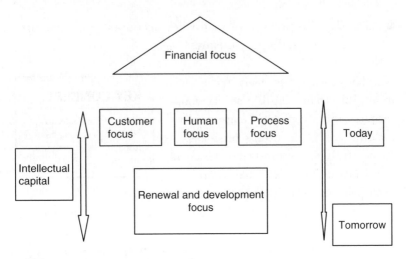

Notes:
Human focus relates to human capital.
Customer focus plus process focus constitute structural capital.
Human capital plus structural capital constitute intellectual capital.
Renewal and development are geared to enhance intellectual capital.

Figure 3.3: Skandia Navigator

(Banks and venture capitalists are more interested in structural capital when they come to make investments.)

The market value of a business, according to Skandia, depends on financial capital + intellectual capital.

> **KEY CONCEPT**
>
> Within structural capital, the main components left behind when the employees go home is the customer capital.

- *Intellectual capital* consists of human capital and structural capital.
- *Structural capital* involves customer capital and organisational capital.
- *Organisation capital* consists of innovation capital and process capital.

- *Innovation capital* consists of intellectual property and intangible assets.

The focus of measurement is on the *renewal and development* of human capital and structural capital. The approach is similar to that of the Intangible Assets Monitor and the Balanced Scorecard. The Navigator also takes into account the external environment within which businesses operate.

An e-business can adopt and adapt the Skandia Navigator to measure the value of its business and the impact of its intellectual capital on future performance. Since its focus is the renewal and development of human and structural capital, this is very appropriate to the nature of e-business.

If the business does not want to pick one of these off-the-shelf methods of measurement, it could devise its own, as long as it considers the following:

- The objectives of measurement.
- What is being measured and why.
- Involve all resources – tangible and intangibles – in the measuring method.
- The method should add value. In other words, monitor the performance and make appropriate adjustments to remain on track.
- Make sure that performance indicators are reliable and appropriate.

The important questions to ask are:

- What are the desired results?
- Who is going to be involved in the measurement process?
- How is measurement going to be done?
- What actions will be taken to close the gaps, if any?

GETTING STARTED: How to enhance intangible assets

1   Invest in technology because it is an enabler. It enables organisations to build relationships among employees and between employees, suppliers and other partners and customers. Technology also plays a key part in capturing the tacit knowledge of employees.

2   Allow your staff to make mistakes and to learn from them. Give them an opportunity to develop and to build their skills. Encourage them to share their knowledge.

3   Capture and build information about customers, competitors and your partners.

4   Empower your staff to make key decisions.

5   Incorporate knowledge management strategy into your corporate strategy.

 PAUSE FOR THOUGHT

◆   Dow Chemical increases annual licensing revenues by $100 million by managing its intellectual assets.

◆   Texas Instruments avoided the cost of building a $500 million wafer fabrication plant by leveraging internal knowledge and best practices.

◆   BP-Amoco focuses on getting people to reflect on what they have done and share learning with others.

◆   The average organisation loses half its knowledge base via staff turnover and customers defecting.

◆   ICL set up a project, 'Valuing Intellectual capital (VIC), and created a new position, Programme Director for Knowledge Management, in an attempt to locate knowledge in the firm.

◆ By looking at the market value, versus book value, a major proportion of growth companies such as Intel, Dell, Microsoft and Netscape are valued way beyond their book value. This gap is the result of their intangible assets.

Key messages

◆ Given the profile of an e-business, the focus of attention should be on intangible assets.

◆ Intangible assets include people, brands, culture, organisational routines and information infrastructure.

◆ Intangible assets are difficult to measure but that does not mean that they should not be measured.

◆ The measurement of intangible assets will reflect the true value of a business.

◆ There are various methods of measuring intangible assets. Some of the key ones are the Balanced Scorecard, the Intangible Assets Monitor, the Business Excellence Model and the Skandia Navigator.

◆ All methods of measurement focus on people and their relationships with customers and business partners.

◆ Intangible assets matter most in e-business relationships. Hence attention should be paid to measuring intangible assets.

Knowledge management is about people

The world of reality has its limits; the world of imagination is boundless. (Jean-Jacques Rousseau)

Overview

It has been said that knowledge is 70 per cent people, 20 per cent process and 10 per cent technology. This chapter deals with the people aspect of knowledge management. It looks at the following:

- Training people in a western culture to share knowledge.
- The importance of open communication in the creation of knowledge.
- Creating a feeling of 'I am OK – You're OK'.
- The value of trust.
- The importance of good leadership, empowerment and motivation in e-business.
- Necessary steps to be taken to bring about best practice in people management.

Knowledge management is a process that involves everyone throughout the organisation. Professor Nonaka, first Xerox distinguished professor of knowledge at the University of California, Berkeley, has emphasised that only human beings can take the central role in knowledge creation. The most important asset of any business, but more so of businesses operating in the new economy, is people – the knowledge workers.

> Business is a human organization, made or broken by the quality of its people. Labour might one day be done by machines to the point where it is fully automated. But knowledge is a specifically human resource. It is not found in books. Books contain information; whereas knowledge is the ability to apply information to specific work and performance. And that only comes with a human being, his brain or the skill of his hands. (Peter Drucker)[10]

According to Drucker all employees of organisations are knowledge workers, whereas some other writers apply the term only to those employees who use substantial information to do their jobs, such as consultants. It does not matter who we categorise as knowledge workers, what is important is to value all employees and to provide motivation and leadership to create and transfer knowledge, whatever the source. An organisation's real knowledge is embodied in the experience, skills, knowledge and capabilities of its individuals and teams.

There are different types of knowledge to be considered when dealing with people. *Embodied* knowledge is action oriented and related to the knowledge of experts. People who are experts in specific systems or website building, for example, have knowledge that is substantially tacit.

KEY CONCEPT

Our people are our greatest asset. This sentiment has mostly been hype rather than reality. For e-business it has to be a reality.

Embrained knowledge is dependent on conceptual skills and cognitive abilities. Entrepreneurs and software consultants have this type of knowledge, which again is mainly tacit.

Then there is *encultured* knowledge, which is gained by working in groups and teams where understanding is shared. In such a situation, tacit knowledge is made explicit and 'new' knowledge is created. An organisation with a collaborative culture encourages the creation of knowledge by fostering collective understanding.

Knowledge that is embodied, embrained and encultured is of immense significance to an e-business because of the dynamism and innovative mindset it requires.

Understanding how knowledge is created

Another classification of knowledge is into tacit and explicit. *Tacit* knowledge is within a person, relating to intuition, perception and thinking patterns. It has a technical as well as a cognitive dimension. *Explicit* knowledge, as the name implies, is knowledge that has been articulated and recorded. These two types of knowledge are inter-related.

According to Professors Nonaka, Umemoto and Sasaki,[11] organisational knowledge is created by interactions among individuals. In such an interaction four modes of knowledge conversion take place: socialisation, externalisation, combination and internalisation.

Socialisation

In this mode individuals get together and openly and freely share their experiences about specific tasks, projects or processes. In this way the tacit knowledge of individuals is transformed into the tacit knowledge of a group.

Externalisation

In this mode tacit knowledge is articulated into an explicit form. For example, individuals in a particular organisation may talk about their experience of configuring a value chain in an e-business they know about. As a consequence of collective reflection, they come up with a model that is specific to the business they are addressing. In this way, tacit knowledge is converted into explicit knowledge, which the business can use to create a new product or provide a new service.

Combination

In this mode the existing explicit knowledge of the individuals or teams is transformed into systemic knowledge, such as a set of specifications for a prototype of a new product. Again focusing on creating a new model for an e-business, the process would involve analysis of various factors and deductive creation of systemic explicit knowledge of the appropriate structure for the e-business.

Internalisation

In this mode explicit knowledge is transformed into tacit knowledge, which is operational in nature. Acquiring specific knowhow comes about because of an individual 'taking in' explicit knowledge and thus acquiring new tacit knowledge. According to experts this mode is triggered by 'learning by doing'.

Organisations like BP-Amoco, Hewlett-Packard, Royal Mail, 3M, Chevron, Dow Chemical, Texas Instruments, Ernst & Young, KPMG, McKinsey, Skandia, Bankers Trust, Microsoft, Sun Microsystems, Amazon and Autonomy, to name but a few, have put in place systems to create and transform knowledge by way of socialisation, externalisation, combination and internalisation. The success of each mode of transformation will depend on the organisation's culture, the way it treats its customers and employees and the way it uses technologies as enablers to facilitate knowledge flows within the organisation and between the organisation and its customers and partners.

These four modes of knowledge transformation are to some extent also national culture biased. For example, in Japanese companies informal meetings often take place outside the workplace when participants chat over sake and a meal. Through this informal process (socialisation mode) tacit knowledge is created.

The level of mutual trust in Japan is higher than in western cultures because of the way businesses are structured. In many cases they are family networks. There is a culture of consensus, collaboration and open communication.

> **KEY CONCEPT**
>
> Employees have to be trained to exchange interpersonal trans-actions and share infor-mation and knowledge.

In the absence of such relationships in western economies, consideration has to be given to the type of training that would promote interpersonal relationships. Such relation-ships are important for sharing knowledge.

Training employees in western cultures to share knowledge

Aspects of training to be considered

In an e-business it is very important to create the feeling of 'I'm OK, You're OK', because the driving force of change within the organisation is employees' talent.

This is a concept that comes from transactional analysis and it is important to train employees in exchanging

	High	Concern for self	Low
High	I'm OK You're OK 'A'	I'm not OK You're OK	
Concern for others			
Low	I'm OK You're not OK	I'm not OK You're not OK	

Figure 4.1: I'm OK, You're OK

transactions and acquiring interpersonal skills. Open transactions facilitate effective communication, which is very
important for knowledge sharing, whereas crossed transactions indicate an 'I am not OK' feeling and stop people
from listening. To generate the 'I am OK and You're OK'
feeling, there has to be a high concern for self and a high
concern for the organisation (see Figure 4.1).

It is the task of a leader to understand this and to see that
employees operate in box A. Those with feelings of 'I am OK
and You're OK' will share their knowledge freely. More
information on this type of leadership is explored in Chapters
5 and 9.

Company strategy toward training should explicitly reflect
three dimensions: structure, products and processes; customer
service and the need to deliver service excellence; and
employee satisfaction.

Communication skills

Training should also be focused on communication. A Johari
Window framework could be used to create a high degree of
knowledge sharing. This model facilitates communication by

	Things I know	Things I don't know
Things she/he knows	Open arena	Blind spot
Things she/he doesn't know	Façade	Unknown

Figure 4.2: The Johari window

using what the parties involved know about themselves and others (see Figure 4.2).

Information about an individual is represented from two perspectives, information known and unknown by self, and information known and unknown by others. Together they form the following four categories:

- *Open arena* – information known by both the individual and others.
- *Blind spot* – information unknown to the individual but known to others.
- *Unknown* – information unknown to both parties.
- *Façade* – information known to the individual but not to others.

Feedback should favourably affect the open arena of the Johari window. The extent to which an individual is willing to share their information and knowledge will affect the open arena category (see Figure 4.3). As more information and knowledge is shared, the blind spot disappears. There will also be no room for façade. However, the blind spot will not disappear completely because not all knowledge can be shared; there will always be a proportion of tacit knowledge that will remain tacit. According to Polyani, we cannot tell all we know.

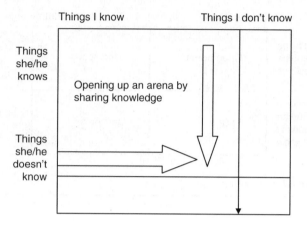

Figure 4.3: Opening up the Johari window

Knowledge creation in practice

Modes of knowledge transformation create knowledge flows within the organisation. These knowledge flows become the lifeblood of the organisation. Businesses that succeed in creating smooth knowledge flows gain competitive advantage; those that create blockages as a result of strategy, culture or structure lose out.

Case study: IBM – an organisation nearly destroyed by knowledge blocks

IBM was overwhelmingly successful for a number of years. It then started losing revenue, from a profit of $6 billion to a loss of $5 billion. More than 200 000 people lost their jobs. In January 1993, John Akers resigned and he was succeeded as chief executive by Louis Gerstner.

IBM's motto was 'Think' and it believed in knowledge creation and leveraging knowledge – so what went wrong?

CONTINUED . . . **Case study: IBM – an organisation nearly destroyed by knowledge blocks**

The knowledge flows within the organisation were blocked by the following:

■ Bureaucratic structure.

■ Very slow decision-making process.

■ Lack of proper empowerment.

■ Mistrust among senior executives.

■ Arrogance in believing that its brand was all powerful and would overcome knowledge blocks.

■ Not properly assessing the changing external environment.

■ Losing key employees and with it their tacit knowledge.

■ Most importantly, not listening to customers.

Gerstner was determined that IBM would create a process to capture knowledge about its customers, processes, and partners. In the years since his appointment, IBM's profits and share prices have recovered. As *The Economist* put it: 'Even more remarkable is the way rivals in the computing industry who were preparing to dance on IBM's grave a little while ago are now falling over themselves to imitate its business model.'

The role of the Internet and modes of knowledge transformation

● The Internet enables sharing of experience about customers' buying behaviour and promotes networks to facilitate communication. It plays a key role in promoting the socialisation mode of knowledge creation. It enables sharing of knowledge among 'virtual' teams and it facilitates widening of the open arena in the Johari Window.

- Designing a way to sell on the web is a reflection of the externalisation mode of knowledge creation.
- Conducting a business through the medium of the Web would be the combination mode.
- Learning a lesson from the experience of doing business through the Internet would be the internalisation mode.

The inter-relationship of modes of knowledge creation

All four modes of knowledge creation are inter-related. The messages gained from these four modes of knowledge creation and transformation are as follows:

- Knowledge has tacit and explicit dimensions.
- Tacit knowledge can be made explicit if an organisation creates an environment to facilitate it.
- Knowledge creation is about communication. It involves interpersonal as well as group communication.
- To articulate tacit knowledge requires an individual to trust the organisation and the leader to motivate individuals to share knowledge.
- Shared experiences, war stories, analogies to promote understanding and learning by doing all are important aspects of knowledge creation.

Individuals' tacit knowledge is the basis of organisational knowledge creation. The key driving force of turning individual tacit and explicit knowledge into organisational knowledge is trust.

Trust me!

Trust is a must for knowledge creation and it has also become a business imperative. It is, as some experts put it, 'the gateway to successful relationships'.

Trust incorporates confidence, expectation, reliance and hope. To trust someone involves expectation on the part of the trustor that the trustee will not abuse the property or information transferred.

Generally in an organisation trust is good to have, but for knowledge-based organisations trust is a 'must have'. Knowledge is power, therefore for one person to pass on part or all of this power, they must expect a positive outcome. Trust is about relationships and as relationships among employees constitute a key aspect of intangible assets, trust has to be institutionalised for the organisation to be a true knowledge-based organisation.

In 1999 Financial Times Management organised a competition to find the best idea for twenty-first-century business. This author put forward the idea that the biggest challenge facing the business world would be institutionalising trust in the organisation. The idea was voted a winner.

In the 1980s and early 1990s many organisations went through a process of downsizing (and in some cases capsizing) and re-engineering, and a number of employees were made redundant. In many cases employees were

> **KEY CONCEPT**
>
> Trust is a matter of the heart. An organisation should win the hearts and minds of its employees.

treated very badly by their organisations. As one executive remarked, 'When my boss tells me "trust me" I get worried.'

Trust has been eroded by leaders who have very little respect for people and who do not understand the importance of talent in enabling an organisation to compete successfully. According to Charles Savage:

We have designed into our companies a culture of distrust. Instead of valuing people, we have fostered a climate where people do not feel valued for what they know or what they can do. We have focused on hands and not heads and hearts. If we want to move into the knowledge era, our biggest challenge is a cultural one.[12]

Trust has to be part of the corporate culture and it has to be manifested by top management. As it has been said, 'Example is not the main thing in influencing others. It is the only thing.'

Trust in the e-business environment

- An e-business needs to reinvent itself continuously in order to respond to market changes.

> **KEY CONCEPT**
>
> Without trust an e-business will be starved of its energy.

- An e-business relies on a network of relationships.
- The success of an e-business is driven by the creation and transfer of knowledge.
- Many e-businesses operate in the virtual world, so people have to establish relationships without meeting face to face.
- An e-business functions by creating partnerships.

Under these circumstances, trust becomes paramount. Robert Bruce Shaw[13] proposes a framework for building trust in which he highlights three key leverage points: leadership practices; organisational architecture; and organisational culture. The trust imperatives, according to Shaw, are achieving results (following through on business commitments), acting with integrity (behaving in a consistent manner) and demonstrating concern (respecting the well-being of others).

Leadership

The task of a true leader in a fast-moving world is to institutionalise trust. *Leadership is not about style; it is about substance.* There is a great deal of rethinking to be done in considering leadership in an e-business.

In order to make trust part of the fabric of the organisation, an e-business leader has to have the ability to:

> **KEY CONCEPT**
>
> E-business leadership is not a question of style but of substance.

- enthuse their employees;
- engage in strategic thinking;
- empower their people;
- create trust throughout the organisation and trust between its employees and its partners;
- understand the importance of knowledge as a source of business energy;
- identify and leverage intangible assets;
- be a coach and a mentor;
- motivate and manage the expectations of their staff;
- be a custodian of corporate governance in the age of the Internet;
- understand that the rules of the game are constantly changing and that they have to be proactive in coaching their team to play;
- know that the models of traditional companies are no longer appropriate and that they need to use the Internet to explore new directions and create a responsive business structure;
- lead not only their staff but also all network business partners;
- be willing to engage in creative destruction, since the e-business requires constant renewal of its business model.

PAUSE FOR THOUGHT

'In order for a company to survive forever, the company must have the courage to be able to deny at one point what it has been doing in the past; the biological concept of "ecdysis" – casting off the skin to emerge to new form. But it is difficult for human beings to deny and destruct what they have been building up. But if they cannot do that, it is certain that the firm can not survive forever. Speaking about myself, it is difficult to deny what I've done in the past. So when such times comes that I have to deny the past, I inevitably would have to step down.' (Mr Kaku of Canon, as reported in a case study prepared by INSEAD, 1992.)

Empowerment

Empowerment was a management phenomenon in the 1980s. As far back as 1983, Professor Rosabeth Moss Kanter of Harvard University emphasised the need for people to work as 'corporate entrepreneurs'.

Empowerment is the act of releasing human energy in order to provide service excellence. It is about creating situations where workers share power and assume the responsibility for making decisions for the benefit of the organisation. Empowerment providing an opportunity to gain achievement, responsibility and advancement.

> **KEY CONCEPT**
>
> Values and trust are pre-conditions of empowerment. Empowerment transforms commitment into contribution.

For an e-business empowerment is very important because decisions have to be made swiftly and the whole organisation has to manage a paradigm shift. Empowerment therefore gives people power to make decisions at the coal face and gets their commitment and involvement.

Empowerment is based on the assumptions that employees want responsibility, that they want to own a problem, that they understand the corporate strategy and that they feel they are trusted.

It can be looked at from both an organisational and an individual perspective. Organisations can empower by sharing open information and creating an appropriate climate and good leadership to facilitate employees making key decisions. Employees, however, need to be convinced that top management means business and that they are trusted. At the end of the day, *people have to empower themselves*.

As we shall see later, continuous improvement is imperative for an e-business. Continuous improvement depends on the involvement of employees and their contribution to enable their organisation to cope with a changing business environment. Empowerment is a key driver in this process.

Benefits of empowerment

- Increased motivation, commitment and energy.
- Improved customer focus.
- Reduced staff turnover.
- Increased innovation.
- Greater flexibility.
- Strong and extensive network relationships.
- Improved individual performance.
- Better ability to cope with change.
- Favourable impact on business bottom line.

There are many stories of organisations that have empowered their people but the initiative did not produce the desired results. Why should such an initiative succeed for an e-business? It is important to understand the causes of failure so that they can be avoided.

Causes of failures

- Top managers are not willing to let go.
- Fear of the new.
- Risk aversion.
- Lack of skills.
- Lack of communication and understanding.
- No clear standards or parameters set.
- Clinging to established ways of doing things.
- A blame culture.

> **KEY CONCEPT**
>
> People will be energised and create a competitive advantage for the company by being very willing to share their knowledge and acquire new knowledge when they:
>
> - have a sense of purpose;
> - are treated with respect, dignity and fairness;
> - apply their skills to meaningful work;
> - are encouraged and given the opportunity to grow.

The three most important success factors for empowerment from the individual's perspective are:

- ability;
- opportunity;
- willingness to take responsibility.

 IMPLEMENTATION CHECKLIST: how to empower

- Share information openly.
- Ensure strong leadership to facilitate empowerment.
- Remove the blame culture.
- Train employees to assume entrepreneurial roles.
- Ensure employees understand the challenges facing the business, especially the e-business if they are involved in it.
- Make sure there is trust at every level of the organisation.
- Establish clear parameters.

Gaining commitment from employees to participate in the knowledge-creating process requires fulfilment of the psychological contract that comes into existence when an employee joins the organisation. Commitment is a two-sided coin. On one side, employees should give their full commitment to the business and subscribe to its strategy and mission; on the other side, the organisation should give its commitment to employability, fair consideration and just treatment. This is the nature of the psychological contract. Failure to satisfy this contract will result into poor customer and employee satisfaction.

> **KEY CONCEPT**
>
> Knowledge is power. In asking employees to share their knowledge, you are effectively asking them to empower their colleagues.

Empowerment in a knowledge-driven organisation: a different perspective

Empowerment has been practised in many organisations for more than two decades. The process, however, has always been top down. The power to make decisions and take responsibility has been handed down from top management to lower levels of management.

Empowerment in knowledge-driven organisations, on the other hand, is a lateral and horizontal process. When employees share their knowledge with their colleagues for the organisation's benefit, they are empowering their colleagues to improve their performance. As more knowledge is shared, more and new knowledge is created.

Knowledge is power. In asking employees to share their knowledge, you are effectively asking them to empower their colleagues. An employee in this situation would want to know 'What's in it for me?'

Elizabeth Lank, programme director of mobilising knowledge at ICL, argues that organisations have to come up with a different structure of reward system to encourage collaboration and knowledge sharing. Some organisations have built knowledge-sharing criteria into their staff appraisal system to demonstrate how much they value this aspect of employee contribution. She also advocates making more information available through enabling technologies and strong and effective leadership to introduce a collaborative culture.

Motivation

What are the motivating factors for knowledge flows within and between organisations?

Management books present us with various theories of motivation. These can be categorised as content theories of motivation and process theories of motivation.

Content theories relate to the needs, drives and instincts that lie behind an individual's behaviour to do or not to do certain acts. The most influential theories of motivation that are categorised as content theories are Maslow's hierarchy of needs and Herzberg's dual factor theory. Some consultants and management development experts consider these theories to be obsolete in the new economy; to think so would be to throw the baby out of the bath water. Just because some of these theories have been formulated more than four or five decades ago it should not be assumed that they are irrelevant in the new economy.

According to Maslow there are five levels of needs that act as motivators. They are:

- *Physiological needs* – food and shelter.
- *Safety needs* – secure environment.
- *Social needs* – friendship, social interaction, sense of belonging.

- *Esteem or ego needs* – respect and responsibility.
- *Self-actualisation needs* – development potential.

One of the criticisms of this theory is that there is no evidence to suggest that all employees can satisfy their higher-level needs, that is, ego and self-actualisation needs. This, however, will not be the case with today's knowledge workers.

Knowledge workers are motivated by esteem or ego needs. They need to develop self-respect and gain the approval of others. They also want an opportunity to develop their full potential in their jobs.

To be motivated knowledge workers therefore need recognition, appreciation, challenge and an opportunity to develop. As Peter Drucker wrote:

The knowledge worker needs a job, to be sure. But only in a genuine and long-lasting depression does the knowledge worker need a job more than the employer needs the knowledge worker.[14]

> **KEY CONCEPT**
>
> In a knowledge-driven organisation, management by intimidation has to be replaced by management by appreciation and trust.

In a knowledge-driven organisation the worker is the owner of the resource. Employees have to be motivated, but at the same time have to motivate one another by sharing their ideas, experiences and knowledge. Esteem and self-actualisation needs will be met by the organisation as well as peer groups.

Maslow's theory and communities of practice

Communities of practice are groups of people informally bound together by shared expertise and passion for their discipline. Some members of a community of practice meet face to face while others keep in touch virtually.

Communities of practice solve problems quickly and transfer best practices. According to Wenger and Snyder,[15] the purpose of communities of practice is to develop members' capabilities and to build and exchange knowledge. The members select themselves as members and the communities are held together by passion, commitment and identification with the group's expertise. This is similar to members wanting to achieve their social, esteem and self-actualisation needs. If such communities of practice come into existence within an organisation, knowledge will be shared freely.

Herzberg's theory

Herzberg's dual factor theory distinguishes between hygiene factors and motivators. According to his theory, factors that cause dissatisfaction at work are not motivators but hygiene factors. These factors are status, interpersonal relations, supervision, company policy, job security, working conditions and pay.

The motivators are recognition, achievement, possibility of growth, advancement, responsibility and work itself. Existence of these factors motivates workers.

The problem of applying this theory to today's knowledge workers is that it is difficult in practice to have a clear demarcation between hygiene factors and motivators. Hygiene factors such as company policy and interpersonal relationships can and do play important role in motivating workers to share knowledge. They have to perceive that the company policy facilitates a practice of sharing knowledge and interpersonal relationships become very important in communicating experience and telling stories.

Process theories of motivation focus on:

- Goal setting.
- Equity theory.
- Expectancy theory.

Goal setting

The basis of this theory is that employees' behaviour is directed towards goals that they have set themselves and that these goals are reflections of their values and desires. Employees will be motivated to contribute to performance if their personal goals are congruent with organisational goals. Goals serve as the motivator.

According to this theory, the goals set by the organisation should be attainable and the process should involve the employees concerned.

In a knowledge-driven organisation specific goals should be set and measured for knowledge sharing among employees and between employees and partners. These goals should be specific and clear. Feedback should be provided concerning goal attainment.

Equity theory

According to this theory, individuals are motivated to maintain fair relationships among themselves and to avoid those relationships that are unfair.

In a knowledge-sharing situation, if an individual feels that an organisation takes advantage of their experience and that the effort they make is rewarded less than other colleagues who do not have as much experience or share as much knowledge, this will affect that individual's behaviour.

An individual's perceived inputs and outputs are compared with their colleagues' inputs and outputs. It is the individual's *perception* that matters.

Expectancy theory

There are three basic elements of expectancy theory: expectancy, instrumentality and valence.

Expectancy

This is an individual's belief that by making a great deal of effort they will accomplish a lot. An individual's expectancy in relation to their effort plays a key part in their behaviour. If an individual feels that no matter how hard they try to create knowledge-sharing efforts, the company will not pay any attention, they are not going to make much effort.

Instrumentality

Even if an employee works hard at sharing knowledge, if their efforts are not going to be rewarded, for example if they have reached the top of the salary scale, there is going to be a lack of motivation.

Valence

This simply refers to the value an individual places on an event or outcome. Even if employees believe that their contribution to knowledge sharing will lead to improvement in the company's performance and that their reward will be commensurate with their

> **KEY CONCEPT**
>
> Knowledge is owned by individuals. When organisations fail to motivate individuals they lose out on gaining knowledge, thus unfavourably affecting the organisation's capability to gain and sustain competitive advantage.

efforts and contribution, they will be poorly motivated if those rewards have a low valence to them. It is the *value* that these employees attach to the outcomes that matter.

The fundamental question 'What's in it for me?' is always there in practice. The answer that will satisfy the individual will depend on:

- What the organisation expects of an individual.
- What an individual expects of an organisation.
- What employees value.
- Whether employees' values are congruent with the organisation's values.

The social centre of gravity has shifted to knowledge workers, according to Peter Drucker. Knowledge workers have new values and expectations. The influential theories of the past still have relevance in a context of knowledge sharing, provided that they are applied selectively.

Employees have to trust the organisation for true flows of knowledge to take place. The human resource policies of knowledge-driven organisations have to understand the aspirations and the values of employees at the time of recruitment, otherwise there will be a mismatch between the values of individuals and the organisation and knowledge sharing will fail.

The challenge facing knowledge-driven organisations is to get employees to motivate one another through a genuine interest in ideas, capabilities and aspirations. There has to be an effective process of empowerment in the sense of knowledge sharing – knowledge is power.

Key messages

◆ Businesses have to understand the process of knowledge creation and transformation.

◆ The knowledge-creation process involves everyone in the organisation.

◆ Technology, such as the Internet, intranets and extranets is only an enabler.

◆ Employees are now knowledge workers and they have their own values and aspirations.

◆ Established motivational theories have some relevance in helping to understand what makes people tick.

◆ Trust is fundamental if knowledge-driven organisations are to achieve superior performance.

◆ Trust has to be made transparent by modern leaders.

CONTINUED . . . Key messages

◆ Leaders of knowledge workers have to have substance, not style.

◆ An effective leader has to create a climate of empowerment to manage the changing business paradigm.

◆ To motivate and manage knowledge workers, a leader has to:

■ provide outlets for their aspirations;

■ empower them to make key decisions;

■ have a flexible structure where smart ideas can be executed very quickly;

■ understand and support the intangible needs of employees;

■ have a greater tolerance for risk;

■ understand that knowledge workers like to work with talented colleagues and want to work in an environment like that of an exciting and winning sports team.

Managing talent

CHAPTER 5

Today's high performers are like frogs in a wheelbarrow:
they can jump out at any time. (Anon.)

Overview

This chapter deals with recruiting and retaining talent.
It considers the following:

- There is a war for talent in the marketplace.
- Top management has to take a direct interest in
  recruiting and retaining talent.
- The role of the Internet in recruitment.
- Knowledge workers have special attributes and their
  needs and aspirations change the employer–employee
  paradigm.
- As an example, Microsoft manages talent by focusing
  on developing competencies.

Knowledge has become one of the key factors of production
and talent is increasingly recognised as the prime source of
competitive advantage. But knowledge resides in people. It is
their experience and tacit knowledge, when transformed and
embedded in innovation and systems, that become organisational knowledge and capability.

Workers in knowledge-driven organisations have to be
managed differently. Resorting to textbooks does not help.

The attributes of knowledge workers

- They are talented.
- They prefer challenges.
- They have their own aspirations and values.
- They want to be managed by seduction rather than intimidation.

> **KEY CONCEPT**
>
> Talent is of the key sources of sustainable competitive advantage.

- They need more freedom and want to be empowered.
- They like to work with talented colleagues.
- They want to control their own career development as long as the organisation they work for gives them a chance.
- They want to be appreciated for what they are rather than what the organisation wants them to be.
- They are mobile – they can simply walk away.
- They like and enjoy the recognition of their peers.
- Even though money is not the main motivator, new recruits expect to be paid very well.

Shortage of talent

In the 1980s and early 1990s, numerous organisations went through the process of re-engineering, restructuring and downsizing and they created massive redundancies. A significant proportion of organisations saw valuable knowledge and talent leaving their organisations. Some organisations treated their people very badly. They did not manage their organisations properly and staff who remained always worked under the threat of 'you could be next'. Loyalty to these organisations evaporated in the process.

Now organisations are beginning to realise that in the context of globalisation and the development of e-business, knowledge matters and therefore there is a need for talented people to enable organisations to win competitive advantage.

However, there is an acute shortage of talent in the Americas, Europe and Asia. There are reports of skills shortages in a number of different sectors of business. But that does not mean that you should employ just anyone. An e-business in particular requires people who are sensitive to change, who can think on their feet and who can innovate and work in a virtual environment but, at the same time, establish good relationships with colleagues, customers and other partners.

It is reported that there are approximately 1.2 million unfilled IT jobs in western Europe. If current trends continue, there could be as many as 1.7 million unfilled jobs in Europe's technology sector in the next three years. According to a survey conducted by PricewaterhouseCoopers (March 2000), of almost 300 companies surveyed, 70 per cent had severe difficulties hiring qualified staff. The study shows that the talent dearth has held down growth rates by about half and that the trend will worsen as businesses look to add up to 30 per cent more staff for e-business-related activity.

According to some researchers, there were 500 000 specialists working in the IT sector in 1999. It is predicted that 1.3 million people would be required to service the industry by 2003.

As a result of the shortage of skills and the war for talent, recruitment is an important item on the top management agenda. It is reported that Bill Gates spends 40 per cent of his time personally involved in the recruitment and induction of recruits.

> **KEY CONCEPT**
>
> Heads of organisations should take a direct interest in the recruitment process and in recruits.

What are the challenges facing an e-business today?

Knowledge-driven organisations today face three challenges:

1 Recruiting talented individuals.
2 Retaining talented employees.
3 Developing talent within the organisation.

Recruitment

There is a shortage of talented individuals. Survey after survey indicate that organisations find it difficult to recruit the type of individuals they need. Such shortage of talent exists everywhere in the world, but in particular where there is an acute need to create new business models and e-businesses to capture the growing market.

Paying workers at the top of the market is not enough. The organisation has to offer intangible benefits that meet the aspirations of new recruits.

 IMPLEMENTATION CHECKLIST: how to recruit

◆ Go for an experienced recruitment agency.
◆ Be sure about the type of talent your business needs.
◆ Keep your options open regarding the age and experience of potential employees.
◆ Be honest and open about organisational aspirations.
◆ Do not make promises on which you cannot deliver.
◆ Get into universities and colleges very early on and identify talent.
◆ Offer recruits work experience opportunities early, preferably in their first year of studies.
◆ Hire people who can and are willing to acquire new skills to perform different jobs should that be necessary in the future.
◆ Bear in mind the untapped pool of female talent, especially those professionals who have decided to stay at home to look after their young children.

◆ Do not forget recruiting talent is a two-way process. As you assess them, they assess your organisation in return.

◆ Don't neglect 'grey hairs'. Some headhunters have found out that some so-called old people have made good heads of start-ups.

◆ The Internet offers a host of opportunities to advertise your requirements. It is reported that Cisco's primary tool for recruiting talent is over the Internet.

◆ Encourage a 'not invented here but I did it anyway' attitude.

◆ Recruit continuously rather than to fill vacancies.

◆ Make it easier for top talent to find your company. Make effective use of your web site. If you do not have a web site, get one.

◆ Give useful information on the web site about your company, products and services.

◆ Make it possible for people to apply directly to you.

◆ Automate your recruitment process. This will reduce the cost and time your organisation spends in recruitment.

The role of the Internet in recruitment

Numerous organisations have started using the Internet for recruitment purposes. The benefits of recruiting on the Web are as follows:

● It extends marketing reach, enabling companies to promote awareness widely.

● It enables companies to deal with a large number of candidates effectively.

● It facilitates the free flow of information between candidates and companies.

● It customises the whole recruitment process.

● Technology manages data.

● Feedback can be given to candidates immediately.

The recruitment business is thriving as a result of the new economy. In the *Sunday Times* Fast Track 100 Awards (3 December 2000), 14 recruitment firms appeared in the list. The top company was Dataworkforce, a telecoms recruitment agency.

Unlocking the power of the whole brain in e-business

E-business is dynamic. It requires the organisation to be agile, networked and consisting of people who can bring about innovation in products and processes continuously in order to respond to changes taking place in the 'marketspace'.

> **KEY CONCEPT**
>
> Understanding brain structure can enhance business performance.

In recruiting for e-business, consider the thinking styles associated with the specialised thinking structures of the brain. According to Ned Herrmann,[16] the brain has four thinking shelves. These are as follows:

- The A-quadrant analyser – logical thinking, analysis of facts, processing numbers.
- The B-quadrant organiser – planning approaches, organising facts, detailed review.
- The C-quadrant personaliser – interpersonal, intuitive, expressive.
- The D-quadrant visualiser – imaginative, big-picture thinking, conceptualising.

Each quadrant has its own decision style. Quadrant A is associated with a logical, quantitative, critical, analytical and factual style. Quadrant B is associated with a sequential, conservative, controlled, structured and detailed style. Quadrant C is associated with an emotional, humanistic, expressive, sensory and musical style. Quadrant D is

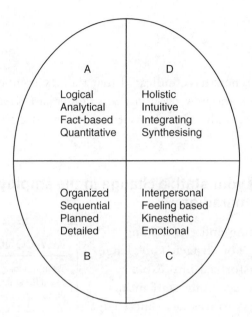

Figure 5.1: The whole brain

associated with a conceptual, synthesising, metaphoric, integrative and visual style.

All these styles are inter-connected, but it is possible to identify a dominance of style. For e-business, the preferred thinking style of a recruit should be quadrant D and C. This will create a good match between the individual thinking style and the requirements of business. Therefore you need people who are:

- willing to experiment;
- imaginative;
- entrepreneurs;
- appreciative of surprises;
- good communicators;
- good listeners;
- supportive;

- intuitive;
- problem solvers.

Some researchers have indicated that the key competencies of employees in the new economy are judgement, creativity, working in a multicultural environment and decision-making skills.

Retaining your staff: a change in the employee–employer paradigm

When creating and transferring knowledge, not all tacit knowledge can be transformed into explicit knowledge. Retaining staff means having access to this tacit knowledge and an opportunity to leverage it.

> **KEY CONCEPT**
>
> Talent is going to be the key differentiator of high-performing business.

More than anything else, it will be markets that decide whether your employees stay with you or not:

> The market not your company will ultimately determine the movement of your employees. Yes you can make your organisation as pleasant and rewarding a place to work in as possible – you can fix problems that may push people toward the exits. But you can't counter the pull of the market; you can't shield your people from attractive opportunities and aggressive recruiters. The old goal of HR management – to minimise overall employee turnover – needs to be replaced by a new goal: to influence who leaves and when. If managing employee retention in the past was akin to tending a dam that keeps a reservoir in place, today it is more like managing a river. The object is not to prevent water from flowing out but to control its direction and its speed.[17]

In a recent survey by the Institute of Personnel and Development, 40 per cent of the employees under 30 see it as normal to change jobs every two to three years. Young people are not keen to commit to one employer for a long period. A retention strategy should take this fact into consideration.

Why do you want to retain your employees?

- Recruitment is a costly business.
- When people leave they walk away with knowledge.
- You want to sustain your training and development investment in your staff.
- Staff turnover affects your customer relationships. Discontinuity in relationships is unsettling.
- Attrition has a domino effect inside your organisation.

> **KEY CONCEPT**
>
> Organisations have to come up with innovative solutions to retain their knowledge workers.

- High staff turnover creates an unfavourable perception of your business to your customers and other partners.
- It is reported that an average of £70 000 is lost per departing employee.
- Staff turnover reduces the rate of product development and innovation.
- High staff turnover creates demotivation and reduces staff morale.
- An extra burden is put on the remaining staff. This in turn affects productivity throughout the organisation.

Case study: One company's effort to retain staff and capture knowledge

Mrs Campbell works for one of the leading consultancy organisations in the trust and tax department. She has expertise in UK, France and US tax requirements and she

CONTINUED ... Case study: One company's effort to retain staff and capture knowledge

has been with the firm for three years. A few months ago she became pregnant and went on maternity leave.

While on leave she was considering alternative employment on a part-time basis that would not involve her in overtime and fee-earning situations. She did not think there could be such a position in the company for her. As a consequence, she managed to get a new job with an established law firm.

She submitted her letter of resignation to her boss who is one of the partners, explaining her reasons for leaving the company. Her boss immediately phoned her and decided to meet her and discuss her change of circumstances. He wanted to retain her and agreed to meet all her requirements. As a consequence, Mrs Campbell withdrew her resignation and decided to stay with the firm on a new contract.

The moral of this story is:

- It is important to make every effort to retain your staff when there is a war for talent.
- It is the responsibility of senior managers to help retain staff.
- Senior managers should take personal responsibility for the loss of staff. Research has shown that a large number of factors contributing to employee retention are within the manager's circle of influence.

In making efforts to retain your employees, do consider a strategy for building commitment. It is important to engage employees' emotional energy and attention. E-business requires employees to be more customer responsive, more flexible, more collaborative, more learning oriented and more team driven. Employees therefore have to be commited. Without such commitment, it would be like a sports team that has star players who cannot work in a team.

According to Greenberg and Baron,[18] there are three types of commitment. *Continuous commitment* involves employees who continue to work for an organisation because for a variety of reasons they cannot leave. They might find it stressful to leave their job or they might have social obligations.

Normative commitment involves employees who continue to work for an organisation because they face pressures from others to do so. Some don't want to disappoint their employer, especially if the company has invested in them in the form of training and development.

Affective commitment involves employees who continue to work for an organisation because they agree with its strategy and they want to be part of it. This type of employee takes the organisation's mission on board and wants to be associated with every stage of organisational development. Leaders in this situation have to articulate and reinforce corporate values.

It is believed that the new generation of workers wants meaning and purpose. They want to work for companies that are in accord with their own value systems. E-business is passion driven and the issue of values is more explicit. According to one consultant:

Most dot.coms are started by one or two people, so the values that drive the business are very personal to them. That is infectious for the people who join. But rapid growth means that you no longer share a coffee with everyone. They quickly realise that they can't instil the passion, the spirit and the values on a one-to-one basis any more. At that point, it becomes really important to articulate their values and communicate them to their people.

The nature of e-business provides an opportunity for leaders to foster affective commitment provided that they value their employees and involve them in organisational development. There is also a downside to e-business, in that if employees are not motivated and they do not feel commited 'burnout' occurs, which does not help the business. Employees become reluctant to share their knowledge and to help organisation transform information into knowledge.

Strategies that some organisations use to retain staff including the following:

- Laundry and car-repair services for their staff.
- In-house gym.
- Dentistry clinic.
- Health care.
- Assistance with child care and elder care.
- Paid parental leave.
- Training and development opportunities.
- Giving staff information and sharing strategic thinking with them.
- Spending lots of time coaching, mentoring and communicating with staff.
- The chance to create and run new businesses or providing incubators.
- In-house venture funds.
- Realistic job expectations.
- Flexible working patterns.
- Work–life balance policies.
- Generous pension schemes.
- Long-term loyalty bonuses.
- Fairness in employment practices.
- Stock options – but be willing to buy back shares if prices fall, and remember that your competitors can easily undo 'golden handcuffs'.

> **KEY CONCEPT**
>
> To retain your staff, you have to pamper them.

Case study: Managing talent and knowledge at Microsoft

Since its founding in 1975, one of the competitive advantages of Microsoft Corporation has been the quality of people. The highly successful software firm goes to extraordinary lengths to hire people with strong intellects and capabilities. According to the authors of *Microsoft Secrets*, a book about the company, one of Microsoft's key strategies is, 'Find smart people who know the technology and the business.'

One of the reasons why Microsoft people need high levels of competence is the fast-changing nature of the industry in which it competes. Microsoft rose to its position of industry dominance in a period of a few years, and Bill Gates, the company's well-known CEO, is determined that the company will stay on top. For example, Gates and other Microsoft executives recently concluded that the company needed to embrace the Internet and incorporate it into virtually all products and services. As a result, software developers and marketers need to be able to acquire new skills quickly.

This unusal attention to human resource capabilities, however, is not restricted to product-oriented personnel. Microsoft's internal Information Technology (IT) group, for example, faces the same pressures to produce software and to adapt to rapid industry change. The IT group consists of over 1000 employees who develop applications, build infrastructure and operate computers and networks. Unlike many firms, Microsoft's IT group does not tolerate 'legacy people' whose skills have become obsolete. If Microsoft's product set includes, for example, OLE (object linking and embedding) technology, then the internal IT group must rapidly incorporate it into the

CONTINUED . . . Case study: Managing talent and knowledge at Microsoft

company's internal systems. The knowledge base for Microsoft IT must always be current.

Therefore, the IT group has focused heavily on the issue of identifying and maintaining knowledge competencies. Neil Evans, the former head of the IT group, is now addressing the issue as a researcher on a National Science Foundation project at the Northwest Center for Emerging Technologies. Chris Gibbon, the current IT director, hired Susan Conway as a Program Manager to take on the issue of knowledge competencies. Conway has developed similar competency programs at Computer Sciences and Texaco before coming to Microsoft.

Conway's goal is to create an online competency profile for jobs and employees within Microsoft IS. A pilot in an 80-person application development group was completed in November 1995 and full implementataion is proceeding. The project, called Skills Planning 'und' Development (thus affectionately known as SPUD), is focused not on entry-level competencies, but rather on those needed and acquired to stay on the leading edge of the workplace. However, shortcomings in the educational system must be addressed by competencies acquired on the job.

The SPUD initiative is being managed by the Learning and Communication Resources group within Microsoft IT, which also has responsibility for training and education for IT personnel. The goal is to use the competency model to transfer and build knowledge, not merely to test it. When Microsoft IT employees have a better idea of what competencies are required of them, they will be better consumers of educational offerings

CONTINUED ... **Case study: Managing talent and knowledge at Microsoft**

within and outside Microsoft. The project is also expected to lead to better matching of employees to jobs and work teams. Eventually the project may be extended throughout Microsoft and into other companies.

There were five major components to the SPUD project:

- Development of a structure of competency types and levels.
- Defining the competencies required for particular jobs.
- Rating the performance of individual employees in particular jobs based on the competencies.
- Implementing the knowledge competencies in an online system.
- Linkage of the competency model to learning offerings.

Developing the competency structure

Before the project began Microsoft had already defined certain competencies, but they were largely restricted to entry-level skills. The Northwest Center was also study-ing entry-level skills for software deveopers, e.g. require-ments definition for a new system. These base-level competencies became known as *foundation* knowledge in the four-type model used in the SPUD project.

Above the foundation level there are *local* or unique competencies. These are advanced skills that apply to a particular job type. A network analyst, for example, might need a fault diagnosis competency for local area networks.

The next level of competencies are *global* and would be present in all employees within a particular function

CONTINUED ... Case study: Managing talent and knowledge at Microsoft

or organisation. Every worker in the Controller organisation, for example, would be competent in financial analysis; every IT employee would be competent in technology architectures and systems analysis.

The highest level in the competency structure is *universal* competencies: universal, that is, to all employees within a company. Such competencies might be a knowledge of the overall business a company is in, the product it sells and the drivers of the industry. A course for all employees sought to provide general knowledge of the software industry and Microsoft's strategies.

Within each of the four foundation competencies there are two different types. Explicit competencies involve knowledge of and experience with specific tools or methods, e.g. Excel or SQL 6.o. Requirements definition competency, for example, is an implicit competency. Implicit competencies involve more abstract thinking and reasoning skills. At Microsoft, the implicit competencies are expected to remain stable over time, although one new one, Web authoring, was recently added. Explicit competencies, of course, change frequently with rapid changes in fortunes of particular languages and tools. Within all four competency types, there are 137 implicit competencies and 200 explicit ones.

Within each type of competency there are also four defined skill levels. A worker might have, or a job might require, any of the levels below:

- Basic.
- Working.

> **CONTINUED . . . Case study: Managing talent and knowledge at Microsoft**
>
> - Leadership.
> - Expert.
>
> Each skill level for each competency is described in three or four bullet points that make the level clear and measurable. The goal of the skill descriptions is to avoid ambiguity in rating jobs and employees.
>
> Defining competencies for particular jobs
>
> Since one of the purposes of the SPUD project was to match jobs and employee capabilities, each job in Microsoft IT had to be rated in terms of the competencies required to perform it.
>
> This task was typically performed by the manager to whom the job would report. There are 40 to 60 competencies in the average job template.
>
> Source: Thomas H. Davenport, Ph.D. 'Managing Knowledge Competencies at Microsoft', University of Texas case study, 1997.

Lessons from the Microsoft case study

- Talent is an important business asset.
- The quality of its people gives a business sustainable competitive advantage.
- Organisations have to put a great deal of effort into searching for the right people.
- The use of the Internet involves developing new skills and updating such skills continuously.
- The organisation has to have a structure that adapts according to market needs.

- Top management has to be involved in change initiatives.
- Organisations should have the courage to eliminate skills that have become obsolete.
- The knowledge base of any organisation is its people.
- Knowledge competencies have to be identified and continuously monitored.
- The profiles of employees have to match the job requirements.
- Employee retention involves providing new skills and competencies to enable employees to stay at the leading edge of the business.
- Training and education has to be a continuous process.
- A lot of effort has to go into analysing competencies and these competencies should be viewed from a broad rather than a narrow business specialism perspective.
- All employees, in addition to their own specialisms, require a broad perspective on the organisation's strategic objectives.
- There have to be clear lines of communication.
- Consideration has to be given to explicit as well as tacit competencies.
- Measurement and monitoring are essential to redefine competencies and to develop staff.

 PAUSE FOR THOUGHT: A memo from the CEO of an e-business to its employees

To: All my colleagues

From: CEO of E-business

Subject: Our value proposition – you are our greatest asset

The business world is changing dramatically and being in a fast-changing environment we need to be innovative and responsive to meet our customers' expectations.

To do so we constantly have to monitor our business propositions to our customers and review our strategy, system, culture and capabilities, in order not just to win competitive advantage but to sustain that advantage.

We very much value your talent and your contribution to every aspect of our business. You constitute one of the key sources of our competitive advantage. In return, we will give you recognition, flexibility and an opportunity to develop your potential and meet most of your aspirations.

In our business we rely on three *E*s: your Energy, your Entrepreneurial attitude and your Enthusiasm. These three elements, reinforced with your competencies, will give us capabilities to achieve superior performance.

We depend on you to generate knowledge and to transfer knowledge in order to enable us to fulfil our strategic objectives. We trust in you to help us to become a successful knowledge-driven organisation and we want you to trust in us to provide an environment conducive to innovative performance.

I am glad you are working for us.

I am sure many people receive such memos regularly!

Key messages

- ◆ People are your greatest asset in today's business.
- ◆ An organisation needs recruitment, retention and development strategies.
- ◆ Explore various avenues of recruitment.
- ◆ Use the Internet to reduce cost and time in recruitment.
- ◆ Prepare a detailed and appropriate brief for the agencies you use. Remember, 'garbage in, garbage out'.

CONTINUED . . . Key messages

◆ Once you have done the recruitment, make sure there is a proper induction process for your staff.

◆ Have training and development programmes in place.

◆ Continuously monitor the skills and competencies of your staff.

◆ Get rid of obsolete skills by retraining your staff.

◆ Have retention strategies in place to stop staff leaving your company.

◆ It is the responsibility of top management to retain staff.

◆ Don't leave it until exit interviews to find out why your staff are leaving. Be proactive.

Capturing knowledge for competitive advantage

CHAPTER 6

No one can whistle a symphony. It takes an orchestra to play it. (H.E. Luccock)

Overview

Knowledge mapping is introduced in this chapter as one of the techniques for capturing knowledge. The chapter discusses:

- How do you prepare knowledge maps?
- What are the basic steps to consider?
- What are the obstacles to be overcome?
- How can basic tools such as continuous improvement, SWOT analysis, quality functional deployment and benchmarking be used to capture knowledge?

The chapter ends with consideration of the knowledge-sharing process at ICL.

Established management techniques such as mapping, benchmarking, continuous improvement and quality function deployment, which became prominent in the 1980s due to total quality management initiatives, can and do play a very important role in capturing knowledge and building knowledge repositories. These techniques are as important today as they were in the 1980s and 1990s and as important to e-businesses as to established businesses.

Knowledge mapping

Once knowledge workers have been recruited, the next step that organisations have to take is to locate the knowledge within the organisation. This is where knowledge mapping becomes very useful. In an e-business environment, decisions have to be swift, projects have to be completed faster than before and skills and competencies have to be continuously improved in order to enable companies to configure their supply chains and fine-tune their strategies. It is therefore a must to know where knowledge is located.

Knowledge mapping is a means of handling knowledge so that it may be used and transferred within the organisation to enhance competitive advantage. It consists of surveys and audits. It explores employees' competencies, it helps the organisation to appreciate how the loss of employees influences intellectual capital and it can assist in recruitment and investment in technology to meet business needs.

A map is a navigational aid that will help you arrive at a desired destination. A knowledge map is a navigational aid for codifying information and experience. A knowledge map shows the sources, flows and constraints of knowledge within an organisation.

> **KEY CONCEPT**
>
> In order to use knowledge you first have to find it.

It is useful – in fact essential – in a fast-changing environment to have a detailed picture of skills, expertise and experience (tangible and intangible forms) within an organisation. This will be a picture of the pool of knowledge that is available to all employees and business partners.

We are used to organisations having organisation charts. Such charts tell us who is where in the organisation and the lines of communication, but they do not tell us the competencies and experiences of the individuals involved. Nor does it tell us where to go and what to do if you are seeking specific information that is crucial to the project you are dealing with, be it product, process or customer oriented.

A knowledge map is an easy-to-use guide showing clusters of knowledge that exist in your organisation. Consultants use knowledge maps to provide a guide to experts in different practices within the organisation. IBM uses Lotus Notes information management software as a knowledge map.

Organisations have to put money and time into creating knowledge maps, but once created these yield very high returns. They can lead to faster decisions regarding product development or winning a major project. Timeliness and cost reductions are two of the key characteristics of e-business.

If a marketing department has built knowledge maps showing the buying behaviour of customers, the product development department can make use of this map to bring about innovative products. The existence of maps in different departments also helps facilitate the flow of information between departments and erode the 'silos' that exist in some business.

Putting information online widens accessibility and it is relatively easy to continuously update the maps. Any department or a team can build a knowledge map.

Vital questions before preparing a knowledge map

- Why do you need a knowledge map?
- Who and what are to be involved?
- What information is normally needed to do the job?
- Who is going to do it?
- How often is it going to be updated and who will do this?
- How is the information going to be categorised?
- How are you going to capture tacit knowledge?

Obstacles to consider

- No time to record experiences.
- No motivation to update information.
- Lack of trust.
- Lack of incentive to share information.
- Organisational politics.
- Suspicion of such collaborative ventures.
- 'My knowledge is my power' attitude.
- 'Not invented here' attitude.

> **KEY CONCEPT**
>
> It is important to remember we are all human.

✓ IMPLEMENTATION CHECKLIST

If you want to build a knowledge map consider the following tips from CIO.com:

- *Start small.* 'Pick an area important to the business, say, customer information and map that first,' advises Thomas

Davenport, director of the information systems management program at the University of Texas at Austin.

◆ *Focus on quality.* 'We were less focused on growth and more on helping people find the contacts they need,' says Martin Stark, strategic planning manager at AT&T in Basking Ridge, NJ.

◆ *Make it easy.* 'The system has to be very intuitive and easy to use, or it won't get universal acceptance,' says John McFadden, vice-president of applications systems development at Chemical Bank in New York. Studies have shown that people are not likely to go much farther than 40 feet from their desks in search of information, so desktop access is a key ease-of-use feature.

◆ *Categorise and define the information.* 'One of the toughest tasks we're faced with is determining what we actually want to pull out into the system,' says Arian Ward, leader of learning and change at Hughes Space and Communications in El Segundo, California.

◆ *Involve the corporate library.* Ward says this is one of the first things he did – both to collaborate with and to learn from the librarians.

◆ *Push and pull information.* While users should always be able to navigate the map on their own, having information sent to their desktops will ensure continued interest. Bruce Young, senior vice-president for emerging technologies and advanced concepts at NationsBank in Charlotte, NC, employs human intelligent agents responsible for dispatching information on a particular technology – voice recognition, for example – to interested parties.

> **KEY CONCEPT**
>
> Listening to other people's advice contributes to building your knowledge base.

Source: C. Hilderbrand, http://www.cio.com/archive/ 070195_map_print_html

At Hoffmann-LaRoche, a pharmaceutical company, knowledge management was used to enhance the bottom line and dramatically reduce product development and time to market. It deployed knowledge maps that involved rewritten guidelines outlining key customer (or regulator) requirements; a question tree charting the questions that customers want answered; contents framing how a company should answer customer questions; knowledge links mapping who should share what knowledge with whom (within the company). There was also a 'yellow pages', listing people who have knowledge and expertise.

 GETTING STARTED

1 We have to stop *devaluing* others in the organisation (discovering weaknesses in others).

2 We have to start *valuing* others (discovering strengths in others).

3 We have to start *adding value* to our organisation (sharing knowledge).

> **KEY CONCEPT**
>
> The future belongs to those who have the willingness to venture into the unknown.

4 We have to start *generating value* by listening to our customers, leveraging our capabilities, using knowledge and establishing networks and partnerships.

Basic steps for mapping knowledge

Assume you are working in a cross-functional team of 20 people and you are working on a specific product development project. The members of the team do not know one another well and they come from different backgrounds and locations.

The first essential information to capture would be the expertise and the capabilities of the team members involved, by preparing a knowledge directory. One framework that could be used would follow the following process.

Scenario one

Stage 1. Who are we? Get each member of the team to write brief information about their qualifications, their capabilities, the projects they have worked on, say, in the past two/three years, or further back if their past experience has direct relevance to the present project. Include the resources they have used and the results achieved.

Stage 2. Ask them to outline their hobbies and interests.

Stage 3. Ask them to write down the things they would like to do for the organisation/team that they are not doing just now.

Stage 4. Share this information among team members (knowledge sharing).

Stage 5. Provide an opportunity for team members to speak with one another to clarify or amplify the information provided.

Stage 6. Put this information online so that all members of the team have access to it. The information can be presented visually indicating links and gaps, types of knowledge and specific experiences.

You now have a knowledge directory of your team members.

Stage 7. Analyse the project at hand in terms of its objectives, the capabilities required and the outcomes. Consider what team members can offer in terms of their experience and competencies and what is needed in terms of the project.

Stage 8. Match project requirements with skill/capability requirements in the light of the information you have (leveraging knowledge).

Stage 9. Once the project is completed, each team member can record their experience of working on the project

highlighting the challenges they faced, the capabilities they have used or could have used and the outcomes.
Stage 10. All information should be put online for others to access and comment on.

You have now enhanced your existing knowledge.

The team has increased its knowledge and updated information on their members to incorporate not just explicit knowledge but also tacit knowledge. The knowledge map created in this process should be continuously revisited and new information added. Note that design and language are key components of an effective knowledge map.

> **KEY CONCEPT**
>
> The practice of continuous improvement is important to update your knowledge plan.

Importance of knowledge maps

- Knowledge maps help create communities of practice.
- Knowledge maps may also identify gaps that exist in terms of competencies and experience. This information can be used to recruit additional team members.
- Knowledge maps may also trigger new business development ideas in terms of experiences, competencies and interests of individuals involved. It is like having an intangible stock of knowledge that can be used to create new products, enter new markets or come up with innovative processes or solutions for your customers.
- Knowledge maps capture important knowledge that can be institutionalised.
- Knowledge maps establish common knowledge among users. Common knowledge facilitates knowledge transfer within the team, department or organisation.
- Knowledge maps help you to stop reinventing the wheel.

■ Knowledge maps save time, thus affecting business costs and helping deliver value to customers.

■ Knowledge maps add value to the whole organisation and its activities.

■ Knowledge maps reflect opportunities for learning and leveraging knowledge.

■ Knowledge maps can also be used as a benchmarking model.

■ Knowledge maps facilitate the analysis of strengths, weaknesses, opportunities and threats facing your business.

Scenario two

Assume that three individuals have got together to start up babyboom.com. They know each other personally but they don't have knowledge of each other's experience and competencies.

Stage 1. Start thinking about business strategy. What kind of business do you want to be in and why?

Stage 2. What objectives are you aiming to achieve and over what period?

Stage 3. What is your business proposition?

Stage 4. How are you going to finance your business?

Stage 5. What is the fall-back position if finance requirements are not met when required?

Stage 6. What kind of supply chain will you require to fulfil your business objectives?

Stage 7. What capabilities will your business need to achieve its objectives?

Stage 8. Prepare a knowledge map of the three individuals involved according to the stages in scenario one.

> **KEY CONCEPT**
>
> Business start-ups can learn a great deal from knowledge maps.

Stage 9. Identify capability gaps from your knowledge map.
Stage 10. Decide how these gaps should be filled and by when.
Stage 11. What if you do not manage to recruit within a defined period?
Stage 12. Prepare a contingency plan.

 PAUSE FOR THOUGHT

Employees of Cap Gemini Ernst & Young can tap into one another's expertise on the corporate intranet to solve problems via a system called Galaxy.

Knowledge maps and SWOT analysis

Many businesses are conversant with the technique of SWOT analysis, which stands for strengths, weaknesses, opportunities and threats that affect organisational performance.

External information about opportunities and strengths is gathered from a variety of sources, including analysing the external environment. Information is also gathered about internal strengths and weaknesses from financial reports, attitude surveys and so on. Looking inside your organisation, the analysis identifies your strengths in relation to your strategy, systems, culture, leadership, processes, products and value. Internal strengths provide sources of organisational capabilities. Weaknesses, on the other hand, reduce your organisational capabilities.

Based on this analysis, organisations assess their capabilities to respond to market needs. For example, an organisation may have the strength of very good network connections with its distributors, or a reputation for dealing with its customers very quickly.

What is important is that through surveys, interviews, customer panels and so on, information is gathered about an organisation's internal capabilities. However, organisations also need to identify the *sources* of strengths and weaknesses. This is when knowledge maps become important.

A knowledge map could be prepared of capabilities and competencies as highlighted in the two scenarios. Strengths and weaknesses in relation to employees' capabilities can be analysed from a knowledge map, which gives information on explicit as well as tacit knowledge. Without a knowledge map, the information gathered will have too many gaps for it to be useful.

Equally, a knowledge map could be prepared of the external environment. A team could be set up to investigate STEP (sociological, technological, economic and political) factors and make a visual representation of the appropriate factors affecting your business. From this information a knowledge map can be prepared that will indicate the impact of external factors on your business, which will enable you to make decisions on articulating various scenarios for strategy formulation.

Knowledge maps used with SWOT analysis provide information on internal and external factors affecting organisational capabilities. This information enables an organisation to measure its intellectual assets.

Knowledge maps and continuous improvement

The concept of continuous improvement is a powerful tool for keeping a company on its toes. It stems from total quality management initiatives and focuses on providing constant and incremental improvement to existing operations.

An e-business's success depends on reducing cycle time and costs, but at the same time continually monitoring to

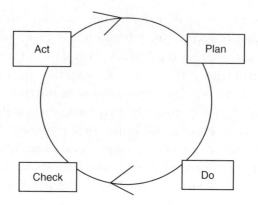

Figure 6.1: Continuous improvement cycle

capture changes and respond to the external environment. Continuous improvement is a must in this situation.

After identifying knowledge gaps in a knowledge map and identifying weaknesses in SWOT analysis, the next step should be to eliminate weaknesses in order to enhance organisational capabilities. In order to do so, the organisation can put a Plan–Do–Check–Act cycle (PDCA cycle) into operation to gather information and take corrective action (see Figure 6.1).

Information gathered and decisions taken along the PDCA cycle should be recorded to create explicit knowledge that people can use to make the organisation more effective. In this way you manage your business by knowledge, not by guesswork or ignorance.

The PDCA cycle can be applied in various situations, including:

- Preparing a knowledge map.
- Skills audit.
- Configuring a value chain.
- Assessing value-adding aspects of business processes.

- Monitoring staff performance.
- Measuring customer satisfaction.
- Considering innovation and learning.
- Assessing degree of empowerment.
- Preparing strategy.

> **KEY CONCEPT**
>
> Continuous improvement is your organisation's fitness exercise.

Continuous improvement involves measurement of key indicators. This generates knowledge of the performance of business assets, tangible and intangible.

Continuous improvement and knowledge creation and transfer

Putting systems into place to create knowledge creation is not enough. There has to be a culture of continuous improvement. For example, any initiative set by the company to transfer knowledge must be monitored by the PDCA cycle and at every stage of this cycle new information has to be taken on board and additional knowledge created.

If the company has decided to create a knowledge map of employees' competencies as Microsoft does, the first stage is to *Plan* what is to be done. At this stage objectives should be set bearing in mind the business requirements and best-practice examples identified.

At the *Do* stage put the implementation into practice. Decide who has to do what, how and when. Set up a baseline measurement system to assess progress. The initial knowledge audit will set the baseline.

The *Check* stage is assessing whether the knowledge-creation process is on track. Consider who is contributing to the process; how much new information is being gathered; how the project under contract is progressing; what value has been added etc.

The *Act* stage is the decision-making stage. Here initial objectives will be revisited and necessary adjustments made.

The corporate culture must support continuous improvement throughout the organisation, putting the focus of improvement on the downstream customer and ensuring that ownership of that improvement is accepted by the process owners and participants.

> **KEY CONCEPT**
>
> Time is of the essence in continuous improvement, especially in the e-world. It has been said that being on track is not enough. If you do not move faster than your competitors, you will be either taken over or run over.

Caution: you cannot approach the PDCA cycle with a checklist mentality. In the case of knowledge creation and transfer, once people 'buy into' the process learning will take place, more confidence will be gained and the process will evolve with confidence and trust.

According to Tom Peters, 'Incrementalism is the enemy of innovation'. This does not mean that continuous improvement should not be undertaken, but that there should be 'breakthrough' thinking concurrently with continuous improvement practice.

Benchmarking

Benchmarking is yet another business technique that is being used to bring in best practice. It is a method of improving business performance by learning from other divisions, teams or organisations how to do things better than before or better than your competitors.

> **KEY CONCEPT**
>
> Benchmarking must be the cornerstone of knowledge-driven organisations.

This is a change area that enables the achievement of best practice. IBM, for example, uses benchmarking as a continuous process of analysing best practice in order to achieve superior performance. Benchmarking has to be continuous and systematic and it should involve evaluation and measurement.

Effective benchmarking can only happen in a culture in which people are prepared to have their thinking challenged and are ready to learn from one another. The practice offers the following advantages:

- It provides direction and impetus for improvement.
- It becomes a stepping stone to 'breakthrough' thinking.
- It identifies best practice.
- It exposes performance gaps.
- It challenges the status quo.
- It fosters 'quantum leaps' changes.
- It breaks an inward-looking focus.

 IMPLEMENTATION CHECKLIST: how to benchmark

Planning

Step 1. Identify a subject to benchmark. For example, preparation of a skills audit or a knowledge map.

Step 2. Identify best practice. This could be located in a different part of the same company or group of companies or in the partners you are dealing with. If necessary, create a model of best practice by involving your employees in coming up with the attributes of such a model.

Step 3. Collect data.

Analysis

Step 4. Structure data into meaningful information to determine gaps. (Remember that structure is raw material; information is structured data; and knowledge is meaningful information, i.e. information within a context.)

Step 5. Determine an action plan to close the gaps and bring about necessary improvements.

Integration

Step 6. Communicate results and analysis. Knowledge creation and transfer result from effective communication.

Step 7. Establish goals.

Step 8. Develop an action plan and prepare steps for implementation.

Step 9. Monitor results and take on board new information.

Step 10. Embed and embody knowledge into systems and procedures as a means of capturing it for future use.

Almost any aspect of business operations can be benchmarked. However, as knowledge is the key driving force in today's business climate, priority should be given to benchmarking knowledge creation and transfer process in order to adopt best practice.

There is now a Knowledge Club in the UK set up by ICL, which can be helpful in benchmarking. Members include the Bank of Scotland and the Department of Trade and Industry.

 Vital questions

. . . before embarking on a benchmarking process

- ◆ Why do we want to benchmark?
- ◆ What is it that we want to benchmark?
- ◆ What specific outcomes are we expecting?
- ◆ Are there best performers to benchmark against and with?

CONTINUED . . . **Vital questions**

◆ What information do we need?
◆ Where would we find this type of information?
◆ Who should we involve in the benchmarking team?
◆ How should we start the process and who should do it?
◆ How do we communicate information and in what format?
◆ Once we get information, what do we do with it?
◆ Are we empowered to make changes?

Knowledge capture and quality function deployment: listening to your customers

Quality function deployment (QFD) is a communication technique for getting product designers to *listen to customers*. The approach enables product designers to take into consideration consumers' needs and transforms tacit knowledge of consumers into explicit knowledge for organisations to leverage in order to win competitive advantage.

A matrix is used to set product characteristics and attributes against consumers' needs (see Figure 6.2). Information is gathered through conducting consumer surveys, market surveys and consulting the salesforce.

Figure 6.2 shows that there is a strong correlation between attribute 1 of product X and consumer need C, attribute 2 and consumer need E, attribute 4 and consumer need A and attribute 5 and consumer need D. According to this information attributes 1, 2, 4 and 5 are very important to enhance in product X because they affect most consumers' needs.

KEY CONCEPT

Quality function deployment has a significant impact on development time and start-up costs.

Product 'X' attributes

Customers' needs*	ATT 1	ATT 2	ATT 3	ATT 4	ATT 5
A	0	0	0	5	0
B	5	3	2	3	0
C	5	2	2	3	3
D	2	1	2	0	5
E	1	5	1	0	0

* Information from surveys, market research, sales force etc.

Scoring: Strong correlation = 5
Weak correlation = 1
No correlation = 0

Figure 6.2: Quality function deployment

A knowledge map could be prepared to present the information visually, which could then be accessed by all designers involved in developing or improving product X.

Some organisations have prepared a QFD matrix using product attributes on one dimension and technology and form of processes on the other dimension. In the matrix, knowledge of the impact of every process on every product attribute can be captured systematically. In Unilever, such QFD frameworks are used to map knowledge, which then is employed to direct research.

Research has shown that use of quality function deployment can reduce development time by 50 per cent and start-up costs by 30 per cent. This is very important for e-business.

Quality function deployment, unlike customer surveys, enables organisations to adopt a proactive approach to customer needs.

In measuring intellectual capital of a business, whether using the Skandia Navigator, the Balanced Scorecard or the Intangible Assets Monitor, traditional business tools such as SWOT analysis or quality function development can be used to gather information on external structure, internal structure, human capital etc. These are the key components to consider when measuring intangible assets.

Case study: Knowledge sharing at ICL

In 1996 ICL established Café VIK in order to encourage knowledge sharing within the organisation. It was a bank of information that could be tapped by employees seeking information on their customers. Within three years of its launch it became part of ICL's culture and its capability.

However, on reviewing such a system it was found that it had information overload. The system was redesigned by streamlining information and to make it interactive to facilitate an effective information system for 'communities of practice'.

In July 1999, Café VIK was relaunched in its new form. Any knowledge community in ICL – defined as a group of people with a business need to share knowledge and information – can create its own space on Café VIK. Café VIK then gives them the ability to manage their membership of that community, publish and archive their own information, hold electronic discussion

KEY CONCEPT

The technology is not what makes knowledge sharing happen – it is communities of people. If there is one lesson to be learned, it is that knowledge management is about connecting people – make sure your technology tools are designed to do the same.

CONTINUED . . . Case study: Knowledge sharing at ICL

groups, poll members on different topics of relevance to the community and post the knowledge and experience profiles of every community member, which can then be searched. The new Café VIK even provides an electronic nagging service. One of the biggest issues with any information repository is the challenge of keeping it up to date. Every piece of information on Café VIK has an owner and a review date. The system automatically checks for the review dates of every piece of information and e-mails the owner to check if the information is going to be updated or deleted.

In the first three months since Café VIK's relaunch, over 100 knowledge communities across ICL have created their space on the information service. With Café VIK the technology is not what makes knowledge sharing happen – it's communities of people. If there is one lesson to be learned, it is that knowledge management is about connecting people – make sure your technology tools are designed to do the same.

Source: Elizabeth Lank, Programme Director, Mobilising Knowledge, ICL, *Human Resources*, February 2000.

Key messages

◆ Creating knowledge is not enough if no one can access it.

◆ A knowledge map is one of the ways of capturing knowledge within the organisation.

CONTINUED . . . **Key messages**

- Knowledge maps can be designed in a visual format and put online for access.
- Knowledge maps can relate to building a knowledge cluster in relation to products, processes and people.
- In practice there are obstacles to knowledge sharing to be identified and attended to.
- Listen and learn from other people's experience.
- Keep it simple and continuously improve the process of knowledge creation and transfer.
- Communicate your intentions.
- Business start-ups can benefit from knowledge maps.
- Use existing business tools and techniques such as SWOT analysis, continuous improvement, benchmarking and quality function deployment to capture knowledge.
- Do your homework. Preparation before execution yields better results.
- Identify best practices in knowledge management.
- Use technology as an enabler.
- Create communities of practice within your organisation.

The role of the Internet in knowledge creation, capture and transfer

Every day the world turns upside down on someone who thought they were sitting on top of it. (Anon.)

Overview

This chapter explores the role of the Internet in knowledge creation, acquisition and transfer. It considers:

- A Cisco case study to show what is happening in practice.
- Hints on building a web site.
- The way the Internet promotes the spirit of entrepreneurship.

CONTINUED . . . Overview

- The use of the Internet for sense-making processes in order to make a start on knowledge management.
- The suitability of the Internet for managing customer relationships.
- Strategic alliances in the Internet era and a checklist for building alliances.

It has been said that no technology in history has spread faster than the Internet. The Internet celebrated its thirty-first birthday in the year 2000. It was created by a system known as ARPAnet, which was used by the United States Department of Defense to make it possible for academic and government computer mainframes to communicate more efficiently.

The current Internet began to take shape in the mid-1980s with the uptake of desktop computing. In the early 1990s it assumed commercial significance and thus started e-business.

The Internet consists of a variety of information and communication components, e.g. e-mail, text documents, databases, discussion groups, news groups, real-time chat, video and audio conferencing and search engines.

KEY CONCEPT

At present experts tell us more than 200 countries are connected to the Internet and 150 million individuals can access the Internet, about 2.5 per cent of the global population.

The Internet is a tool and its biggest impact is *speed*. It delivers speed of deliberations, transactions and information.

It is conquering the world. At present the experts tell us that more than 200 countries are connected to the Internet and 150 million individuals can access the Internet, about 2.5 per cent of the global population. *Fortune* magazine ran a story to show how the Internet has penetrated Europe's most remote spots – geographically (Lapland) as well as demographically (the homeless) – libraries in Budapest, for example, provide free access.

Countries that have advanced telecommunications infrastructures are likely to have faster and more reliable Internet access. According to various research studies,[18] there are 56 million Internet users in the USA and nearly 41 computers per 199 inhabitants; over two million users in Brazil and just under three computers per 100 inhabitants; nearly 11 million users in Germany and just under 26 computers per 100 inhabitants; nearly two and a half million users in Australia and about 36 computers per 100 inhabitants; about one and a half million users in China and just under one computer per 100 inhabitants.

What are the business implications?

According to information provided by *CIO Web Business* magazine (1 May 1999):

Understanding country-to-country variability can help a business prioritize its efforts. In Western Europe, for example, Forrester Research's Don DePalma puts Germany and the United Kingdom at the top of the list of countries to target with a Web effort. Those countries already deliver close to half of Western Europe's online revenues . . . France, Italy, Spain, Austria and Ireland will take a few more years to heat up, he says. In Eastern Europe, Poland, the Czech Republic, Hungary and Slovenia are among the more interesting countries to consider since they have quickly moved to more open economies.
   In Asia, Hong Kong is an obvious choice because of its fibre-optic-rich telecommunications infrastructure.

> **KEY CONCEPT**
>
> Understanding country-to-country variability enables businesses to prioritise market penetration.

The Internet links disparate computer types and a variety of formats into one network. The network then provides the glue for the internal workings of a company. It connects with a web of partners, which is very important for an e-business.

Case study: Syndication: the emerging model for business in the Internet era

'There is no question that the Internet is overturning the old rules about competition and strategy. But what are the new rules?

Many of them can be found in the concept of syndication, a way of doing business that has its origins in the entertainment world but is now expanding to define the structure of e-business. As companies enter syndication networks, they'll need to rethink their products, relationships, and even their core capabilities . . . Although few of the leading Internet companies use the term "syndication" to describe what they do, it often lies at the heart of their business models.

Look at E*Trade. Like other on-line brokerages, E*Trade offers its customers a rich array of information, including financial news, stock quotes, charts and research. It could develop all this contents on its own, but that would be prohibitively expensive on its own and would distract E*Trade from its core business: acquiring and building relationships with on-line customers. Instead the company purchases most of its content from outside providers – Reuters and TheStreet.com for news, Bridge Information Systems for quotes, BigCharts.com for charts, and so on. These content providers also sell, or syndicate, the same information to many other brokerages. E*Trade distinguishes itself from its competitors not through the information it provides but

CONTINUED . . . **Case study: Syndication: the emerging model for business in the Internet era**
through the way it packages and prices that information. Just like a television station, it is in the business of aggregating and distributing syndicated content as well as providing other in-house services such as trade execution.' Source: Reprinted by permission of *Harvard Business Review*, from 'Syndication: the emerging model for business on the Internet era' by Kevin Warbach, May–June 2000, p. 85. Copyright © 2000 by the President and Fellows of Harvard College; all rights reserved.

Capabilities of the Internet

- The Internet facilitates the spread of information.
- It creates a market where buyers and sellers come together. Cisco, it is reported, sold $5 billion in goods over the Internet in 1998.
- It facilitates human interaction, thus enabling the transfer of information and the creation of knowledge.
- It does not distinguish global and multinational companies and medium and small companies.
- It enables companies to reinvent themselves.
- It offers significant marketing opportunities to start-ups.
- It is being used to manage inventory very effectively.
- It enables organisational resources and capabilities to be stretched strategically.
- It gives consumers pricing information. It shifts the balance of power from business to consumers.
- It slashes time and costs out of the supply chain. It is reported that Eastman Kodak saves about $12 million a year on postage, printing and paper costs by using the Internet.

- It triggers off innovations in software, communication technologies and the way organisations deal with suppliers, manufacturers and customers.
- It provides global reach in marketing. It transforms the marketplace to the marketspace.
- It enables organisations to source talent and people to source information on organisations.
- It enables networking and effective knowledge creation.
- Consumers can shop 24 hours a day and from any location.
- It affects the creation and management of brands.
- It is condensing the process of product development and production. Some companies have located product development activities and production processes in different locations with different time zones, which means that products can be developed, produced and marketed in a very short time scale.

> **KEY CONCEPT**
>
> The Internet enhances your organisational capabilities.

- It enables one-to-one marketing. Whereas mass marketing requires product managers to sell one product at a time to as many customers as possible, one-to-one marketing requires customer managers to sell as many products as possible to one customer at a time.
- It shifts the emphasis from product to customer.
- It promotes economic growth. According to some experts, the Internet will add billions of dollars to US GDP.
- It enables the creation of a borderless organisation.

Vital questions

. . . when building a web site

- Is your site fast and user friendly? Remember that your competitor's site is only a click away.

CONTINUED . . . **Vital questions**

- Does it add value for your customers?
- Is information updated regularly? Continuous improvement is a must for an effective web site.
- Does it incorporate adequate customer support?
- Is it too complicated? Ill-fated Boo.com's web site used highly advanced software, which led to technical problems. Many customers found that they could not use the web site because their computers were not sophisticated enough.

The Internet and the new business model

In the traditional model, the value chain is presented as sequential processes involving numerous activities (see Figure 7.1). All these activities and different processes are linked by telephone, faxes, e-mail and computers.

The new model is based on a value chain that deals in concurrent activities embedded in various processes. The underpinning enabling technology of this new model is the Internet, intranets and extranets.

> **KEY CONCEPT**
>
> E-businesses do not have value chains as such but value networks.

It is this concurrent characteristic of the model that affects the time and cost of running a business. In a sense, e-businesses do not have value chains as such but value *networks*.

Dell computer, for example, has a build-to-order business model that was initially based on telephone orders by its customers followed by faxing purchase orders. This was a very efficient supply chain model. Dell now transacts its business over the Internet. Its supply chain has reduced the

From sequential value chain model:

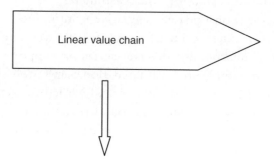

To concurrent value chain model underpinned by the Internet:

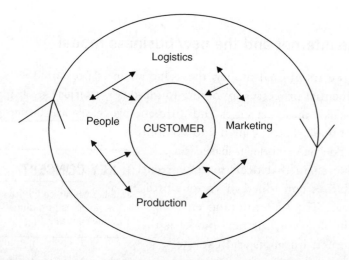

Figure 7.1: Value chain of the new business model

speed of delivery and it offers better customisation of service. Dell's suppliers get an inside look at the company's inventories and production plans, and they receive constant and immediate feedback on how well they are meeting delivery criteria.

Case study: the Internet and the new business model – Cisco

By using the Internet and its intranet Cisco has built a web of partners, making the constellation of suppliers, contract manufacturers and assemblers look like one company – to the outside world. Via the company's intranet, outside contractors directly monitor orders from customers and ship the assembled hardware to buyers later in the day – often without Cisco even touching the box. By outsourcing production of 70 per cent of its products, Cisco has quadrupled output without building new plants and has cut the time it takes to get a new product to market by two thirds, to just six months.

The network also is Cisco's primary tool for recruiting talent, with half of its applications for jobs coming over the Net. When an employee wants information about a company event or health benefits, or needs to track an expense report, the network is the place to go to at Cisco . . . 'We are,' says [CEO] Chambers, 'the best example of how the Internet is going to change everything.'

Source: *Business Week*, 31 August 1998, p. 57.

The Internet and the spirit of entrepreneurship

The Sunday Times, in partnership with Bathwick Group, a new economy consultancy, has created the *Sunday Times* e-league. This is designed to identify Europe's 100 most exciting private companies that use the Net as an integral part of their business. Forrester Research estimates that the European e-commerce market was worth £800 million in 1998 and predicts that it will rise to £2 billion by 2003.

The companies in the league have to make their living through the Internet. They must not be quoted or controlled by quoted companies and they must have their headquarters in Europe.

Companies are evaluated according to their strengths and weaknesses in the following areas:

- Management.
- Business vision and mode.
- Technology infrastructure.
- Financial and user statistics.
- Market reach.
- Marketing and customer relationships.
- Staff and culture.
- Supplier and partner relationships.
- Information and knowledge management.

The top ten e-businesses in the Sunday Times e-league at the time of writing are:

1   Band-X.com (broadband bandwidth exchange).
2   Mondus.com (e-business benefits to small and medium-size businesses).
3   deal4free.com (online foreign exchange trader).
4   Jobserve.com (recruitment company).
5   silicon.com (online IT news and television).
6   WGSN.com (fashion industry information).
7   beenz.com (online loyalty scheme).
8   Moreover.com (global news site).
9   Sportal.com (sports portal).
10 Vavo.com (portal for 'silver surfers', over-45s).

(The e-league is updated regularly and available free at www.bathwick.com/ir/eleague.)

According to the Bathwick Group,[19] a study of the league as it stood in August 2000 reveals the following trends:

- Only 29 of the e-league companies are in the business-to-business market, while 41 operate in the business-to-consumer market.
- Many of the e-league founders have superb qualifications; 36 per cent have MBAs.
- The Internet remains a sector for young people. Some 43 per cent of e-leaguers are aged between 30 and 34.
- Britain is the centre of dot-com innovation (all top 10 companies above are British).
- The Internet appears to have attracted few female entrepreneurs.

> **KEY CONCEPT**
>
> Forrester Research estimates that the European e-commerce market was worth £800 million in 1998 and predicts that it will rise to £2 billion by 2003.

Digital Britain

The Digital Britain awards were instituted by Microsoft and other sponsors. There are five categories of awards. They are.

- Knowledge Management Business Awards.
- Knowledge Management Technology Awards.
- E-Commerce Awards.
- Public Sector Awards.
- Microsoft Awards.

The award for 'Best use of IT for enhanced innovation' (judging criteria: time to market; product quality; customer feedback) went to TWR Group, which 'provides engineering services together with car design and development worldwide. The entry stood out for its commitment to continuous innovation and the way it has brought the organisation closer to the customers. TWR combined innovative and advanced technologies to help its customers cut the lead-time for car development by 20 per cent. The company showed high quality knowledge management through its e-collaboration initiative.'[20]

The e-commerce award for 'Best consumer e-commerce web site' (judging criteria: uniqueness of customer proposition; ease of use; proven effectiveness) went to Iceland.co.uk: 'Iceland Foods set out to build a fully integrated nation-wide Internet grocery home shopping service that would utilise its existing store/home delivery infrastructure and attract new customers. The judges commended this project as a good example of how to deliver an effective "clicks and mortar" strategy.'[21]

Another sector of organisational innovation is Internet sharedealing services. While there were only three dedicated Internet sharedealing services on offer to UK investors at the end of 1999, the figure was closer to 20 in 2000.

According to *The Investor*, Charles Schwab Europe claims to be the largest online broker in the UK and in just over two years, since it launched its online dealing service, it reports having over 93 000 online customers representing over 120 000 online accounts, or 70 per cent of the firm's total business. This is an incredible achievement in a very short period.

Business Week (22 March 1999) offers the following survival guide for electronic business:

1 Reengineer your company.
2 Throw out the old business model.
3 The buyer always wins.
4 Hold your customer's hand.
5 Go ahead, farm out those jobs.
6 No web site is an island.
7 Create an online sense of community.
8 Follow the money.
9 A web of nerds? Don't believe it.
10 Log on boss.

Intranets and extranets as enablers

The term intranet describes a technological infrastructure employing Internet open systems standards and protocols to implement a corporate network. Companies use intranets to distribute information and speed data among offices, divisions and branches. Intranet activities usually take place behind secure 'firewalls' so that only authorised users have access. An intranet is a very effective tool of managing knowledge within the organisation.

An intranet opens up significant opportunities for accessing, sharing and managing information. It therefore reduces cost by saving time and resources in acquiring information. Organisations use an intranet for such tasks as:

- Daily briefing of staff.
- Providing project management database information.
- Giving information on policies and procedures.
- Monitoring orders from customers.
- Other supporting technologies, knowledge-based systems, groupware and document management software form a family of technologies enabling knowledge sharing and transfer.

When the company makes its internal network or intranet accessible to selected partners, the intranet becomes an extranet. Avis Europe, for example, has developed an extranet to allow licensees in different geographic locations to connect to its mainframe-based car retail reservations systems, marketing and sales at Avis Europe.

The Internet and knowledge management

As we have seen, knowledge is the key driver of all businesses in the new economy. To build knowledge requires raw material: data. The data is structured to convert it into meaningful information, which in turn is put into a context to create knowledge.

The Internet enables an organisation to gather as much data as possible on customers, suppliers, products and processes. Various software can be used to transform this data into meaningful information. For example:

> Software from vendors such as Autonomy Inc. features intelligent agent technology to get around the principal barrier to knowledge management applications – the fact that people don't want to interrupt their busy workdays to feed knowledge management applications with the necessary information about their areas of expertise or their solutions to a particular system.
>
> 'It's unrealistic to expect employees to spend a lot of time categorising or tagging documents that others might find useful or filling out elaborate questionnaires identifying their areas of expertise,' says Autonomy Chief Executive Officer Michael Lynch. 'Our goal was to make the process so automatic that effective knowledge management becomes almost a by-product of normal business functions.'
>
> To make each employee's knowledge base accessible to others, Autonomy's Knowledge Management Suite uses a profiling system that automatically identifies the ideas in the documents and e-mail messages the person has submitted to the system and the topics followed in Autonomy's filtered news feed.'[22]

Case study: Becton Dickson network lets employees share knowhow online

At Becton Dickinson & Co. Roberta Smigel has designed an intranet for one of corporate communication's trickiest challenges: knowledge management.

The value of high-tech companies such as Becton Dickinson, a $3 billion maker of medical supplies and

> **CONTINUED ... Case study: Becton Dickson network lets employees share knowhow online**

devices, predominantly lies in the knowledge of its employees.

A year ago, the Franklin Lakes, NJ, company cast Smigel, its World Wide Web business content manager, and corporate webmaster Matthew Bramble as ring-leaders; together the two manage internal committees, an external development firm, and the expectations of upper management in developing the intranet.

Smigel sold the idea of creating knowledge-sharing applications that capture the combined wisdom of the company's more than 19 000 employees. One example is a technical database of best practices. This database is populated by information written by employees and serves as a contact resource and corporate technical encyclopaedia.

Using a database of expertise, anyone at the company can find an in-house expert in plastic injection molding in a few key strokes. Likewise, information on clinical microbiology, another core competency of the company, is readily available online. 'We need to retain knowledge, but also be able to learn from each other,' Smigel says.

Until the advent of an intranet, employees had no systematic way to share knowledge among departments. Committees made up of departmental web-site develop-ment staff, IS employees, and marketing managers decided what information would be most useful to other areas of the company.

Source: Llan Greensberg, *Information Week*, 5 October 1998.

Uses of the Internet in knowledge management

The Internet can facilitate the performance of various key activities necessary for knowledge creation and knowledge sharing. These activities are:

- Capturing data and information.
- Mapping networks of experts.
- Sharing knowledge and best practice.
- Recording experience.
- Embedding knowledge in products, processes and people.

There are many knowledge tools available in the marketplace such as video conferencing, groupware, electronic data interchange, shared databases and other knowledge-based systems. Here we focus attention on the Internet as an enabler for knowledge sharing and creation.

- The Internet is very valuable for getting information from various experts globally. Internet functions such as FTP (file transfer protocol) and the World Wide Web provide easy access to the information products and services of various institutions.
- Information can be obtained via discussion groups and news groups.
- The Internet can also give access to published information on various companies and industrial sectors.
- The Internet also plays a significant role in facilitating customer interaction. It enables a business to capture valuable data, which the organisation can structure in a meaningful way to create business information on its customers. A one-to-one relationship can be created by sending regular e-mails on the status of orders and on other products. The organisation can analyse responses and build a good repository of information on its customers.

■ The Internet enables organisations to get rid of islands of information.

Knowledge creation and sense making

The starting point for managing knowledge is a sense-making process. This involves gathering and interpreting a body of information potentially relevant to a problem. The process includes:

- Information gathering.
- Analysis.
- Synthesis.
- Sharing.
- Reuse.

KEY CONCEPT

The sense-making process enables data to be transformed into structured information.

 IMPLEMENTATION CHECKLIST: the sense-making process

Information gathering

◆ Gather information on who does what, how and where. Identify the key players and the expertise necessary to undertake your project.

◆ Contact people for more information and to 'mine' tacit knowledge.

◆ Record all the information you have collected.

Information analysis

◆ Find out what you have and how you should categorise and interpret the information.

◆ Categorise information according to your needs.

◆ Analyse information. Consider the kind of information you have and examine its significance for your work or the project in hand. Interpret it.

◆ Ask if you need to follow up any information in order to understand its usefulness.

◆ Identify any common themes underpinning all the information you have gathered.

Synthesis

◆ Determine the result of your analysis.
◆ Record the information.

Sharing

◆ Decide how to structure the information to facilitate sharing.

◆ Share the information with your colleagues and team mates.

Reuse

◆ Do not reinvent the wheel. Reuse the information gathered and turn it into knowledge asset to be used and reused.

The Internet and your customers

Many e-businesses focus attention on gaining customers rather than retaining them. To retain your customers you have to convert your processes to a customer orientation. Answer these questions:

> **KEY CONCEPT**
>
> To retain your customers you have to convert your processes to a customer orientation.

● What is your value proposition to your customers?
● Why do they do business with you?
● What is it you do better than your competitor that the customer perceives as valuable?

This could be one of the following.

Product/service innovation

- You continuously invent new products/services.
- You continuously enhance your brand image to achieve a position of dominance.

Operational excellence

- You are efficient in your networking relationships embedded in your supply chain.
- Your service is user friendly and hassle free.

Customer affinity

- You customise your product/service to satisfy customer needs.
- You provide a total solution for the customer wrapped around your product/service.

You have to be as good, if not better, than your competitors at all three of these value propositions in order to succeed.

Ten years ago consultancy Bain and Co. did some research on customer loyalty and retention. The message of its research findings was that increasing customer retention rates by 5 per cent increases profits by 25 to 95 per cent. This message is still just as appropriate.

Frederick Reichheld and Phil Schefter applied the same method of analysing customer loyalty and retention that they had used previously for traditional businesses to analyse customer life-cycle economics

> **KEY CONCEPT**
>
> To gain the loyalty of the customers, you must first gain their trust.

in several e-commerce sectors. They found classic loyalty economics at work:

> At the beginning of a relationship the outlays needed to acquire customers are often considerably higher in

e-commerce than in traditional retail channels. In apparel
e-tailing, for example, new customers cost 20 per cent to 40
per cent more for pure-play Internet companies than for
traditional retailers with both physical and on-line stores.
This means that the losses in the early stages of relationships are larger . . . the Internet is a powerful tool for
strengthening relationships, but the basic laws and rewards
of building loyalty have not changed.[23]

The Internet and strategic alliances

British Telecom signed a global content alliance with
Yahoo!, the online media company, to provide a model
Internet service. (*The Times*, 9 September 2000)

With the Internet it has become easier for a company to ally
itself with others to outsource, co-brand or enter new
markets. Alliances will become the Internet culture of the
new millennium. Because it is difficult to do long-term
planning in the Web-based business, alliances are one of the
key strategic avenues for consolidating the business.

The fast-changing world makes some core competencies
obsolete very quickly. One way of acquiring new competencies is to forge alliances. Alliances are also imperative
for new business models.

Alliances involve competitors and multiple partners and
take different forms, such as joint ventures, strategic
partnerships and co-branding.

Take Cisco as an example
again. CEO John Chambers
believes that partnerships are
the key to the new world
strategies of the twenty-first
century. Cisco has a partnership arrangement with
Microsoft that has resulted in

KEY CONCEPT
Strategic alliances come into exis-tence because the e-world demands a speedy response; businesses operate in a turbulent marketplace; produce life cycles are disappearing; and new competencies become obsolete quickly.

the creation of new technology that makes networks more intelligent. Cisco measures the success of every acquisition first by employee retention, then by new product development, and finally by return on investment.

According to McKinsey, Web-based strategic alliances are different from conventional ones in at least three respects:

1 They involve a much larger and more varied group of companies.
2 They rely on much more informal business relationships and co-ordination mechanisms than the usual detailed legal arrangements.
3 They require leadership by one or two companies to define standards for all members and create incentives that attract more companies to the alliance.

Why do companies forge strategic alliances?

- To improve competitive positioning.
- To form networks that represent the core of the value chain.
- To achieve revenue and cost objectives.
- To acquire new competencies.
- To promote effective marketing.
- To co-brand a business.
- To enable them to provide one-to-one marketing.
- To achieve economies of scope.
- To co-operate on research and development.
- To give the business a global dimension.
- To survive in the marketplace.
- To achieve transfer of knowledge.
- To consolidate business activities.

Britain's top three providers of online wedding services exchanged vows on September 23, 2000 to create Europe's

biggest Internet wedding specialist . . . The deal reflected the need for rationalisation among B2C players, many of whom were running out of money. (*The Times,* 22 September 2000)

 PAUSE FOR THOUGHT

Jungle.com (a computer store launched in August 1999), one of the most visited online retailers in Britain, was sold for £37 million in September 2000 to Great Universal Stores. The reason for the sale was lack of money: Jungle.com could not secure further credit to keep the company afloat.

According to *The Times,* 'One of the main problems for e-retailers which sell to consumers, rather than to other businesses, is that the costs of marketing and advertising are very high. This means that these companies have a very high "burn rate" – a euphemism for "spending other people's money very quickly".'

This burn rate is the fundamental cause for many mergers and acquisitions online. It was also the reason behind the much-publicised demise of another online retailer, Boo.com, in May 2000.

The new game for the new economy

In the old economy the language of competition in business was the language of war (making a killing, beating the competitors, locking in suppliers). What is increasingly happening with the development of e-business is that the language of competition is being transformed into a language of collaboration and relationships. Collaboration creates synergy and enhances value for customers. Collaboration prompts the formation of alliances.

IMPLEMENTATION CHECKLIST: building successful alliances

◆ Alliances are about relationships. Foster good relationships with your alliance partners.
◆ Trust your partners.
◆ Choose your partners carefully.
◆ Alliance building is a two-way process: it involves 'give and take' relationships.
◆ Relationships take some time to foster, so have patience.
◆ You need top management commitment to forge an alliance.
◆ Analyse and consider your partner's culture. Most alliances fail because of culture clash. There has to be consistency between strategy and culture.
◆ Look into your partner's values. They have to be consistent with your values for proper bonding to take place.
◆ Consider doing due diligence on intangible assets and especially competencies and talent within the partner's organisation.
◆ Establish relationships with your partners.
◆ Establish a collaborative and tolerant culture.
◆ Most alliances fail at the implementation stage, so consider how you are going to implement your alliance strategy.

> **KEY CONCEPT**
>
> According to analysts deal making will continue for some time to come. The Internet is a great place to experiment.

◆ Build alliance capabilities within your organisation.
◆ Align alliances with your strategy.
◆ Invest in the technology infrastructure to make alliances work.
◆ Do not introduce sophisticated technology for the sake of it. What matters is not structure but content. Technology has to be user friendly and you must leverage knowledge through technology.

◆ Remember that the consumer expects end-to-end quality. Make sure that alliances enhance the quality of your value chain.
◆ Use alliances to build skills.

Key messages

◆ The Internet is catching the imagination of people all over the world.
◆ Some 2.5 per cent of the world's population has access to the Internet.
◆ This creates an opportunity to create business on the Internet to gain global reach.
◆ To create such a business requires a new mindset and new way of doing business.
◆ The new model has to leverage the Internet to create networks and relationships with customers and all other partners.
◆ An organisation doing business on the Internet has to consider speed, cost and value added when building a web site.
◆ The Internet is also a very effective tool for capturing knowledge, which is the core driver of e-business success.
◆ Using knowledge enables businesses to capture customers. Gaining customers is important, but even more consideration should be given to retaining these customers.
◆ The Internet culture prompts the creation of strategic alliances. For most business-to-consumer organisations, alliances take place because start-up e-businesses cannot sustain the financing of marketing and advertising costs.

Knowledge and innovation

Information plus intelligence is knowledge. Knowledge plus imagination is innovation. (Sultan Kermally)

Overview

Knowledge is the source of innovation. This chapter highlights the following aspects of innovation:

- The role of knowledge brokering.
- Incubators, their role and guidelines for their establishment.
- Promoting innovation in your organisation.
- Transforming 'bricks' into 'clicks' business by innovation.
- The role of the Internet in innovation.
- Survival guidelines for e-business.
- A brief glimpse of digital Britain.

Innovation is the specific tool of entrepreneurs, the means by which they exploit change as an opportunity for a different business or a different service.

KEY CONCEPT

Innovation = knowledge + application + environment.

It is capable of being presented as a discipline, capable of being learned, capable of being practised. Entrepreneurs need to search purposefully for the sources of information, the changes and their symptoms that indicate opportunities for successful innovation. And they need to know and to apply the principles of successful innovation.[24]

So wrote Peter Drucker in 1985. One of the key sources of innovation is knowledge. It is the application of knowledge that brings about innovation. When new knowledge is created in the organisation, it becomes a resource and a source of innovation. The application of the knowledge reflects the capability of the organisation and the outcome brings about innovation. It is the application of knowledge that enables the organisation to gain and sustain competitive advantage.

Knowledge and innovation have two-way relationship. Knowledge is a source of innovation and innovation in turn becomes the source of new knowledge. The cycle of knowledge–innovation involves:

- creation of knowledge;
- application of knowledge;
- invention – bringing into being;
- diffusion of invention;
- innovation;
- new source of knowledge;
- application of this knowledge and so on.

Only an organisation that has a built-in knowledge–innovation cycle will be ahead of the winning game. Innovation is the product of:

> **KEY CONCEPT**
>
> Only an organisation that has a built-in knowledge–innovation cycle will be ahead of the winning game.

- Gathering information.
- Transforming information into knowledge.
- Sharing this knowledge.
- Embedding the knowledge into products, and processes.

- Bringing the products and processes into being (invention).
- Using invention – innovation.

Innovation creates new knowledge and it is shared in a tangible format. Successful innovation usually follows the following sequential of decision-making process:

KEY CONCEPT
Innovation, therefore, is about managing knowledge in the business.

- Idea generation – ideas are the raw material of product, processes and organisational innovation.
- Analysis – examination of the feasibility of innovation.
- Decision to adopt.
- Implementation.

The original idea on which innovation is based does not have to be new. Andrew Hargadon and Robert Sutton make the point that innovation is about knowledge brokering.[25] They say that the best innovators systematically use old ideas as the raw materials for one new idea after another. The innovators also come up with new ideas. These ideas have to be kept alive and one of the ways of doing this is to record the ideas and share information on who knows what. (Knowledge maps can play an important part here.)

> An effective broker develops creative answers to hard problems because people within the organization talk a lot about their work and about who might help them to do better. Companywide gatherings, formal brainstorming sessions, and informal hallway conversations are just some of the venues where people share their problems and solutions.[26]

If these ideas are not recorded, the business loses the knowledge – it walks away with the person leaving the organisation. This is why it is important that the organisation puts in the mechanism and fosters the culture to record and share knowledge so that tacit knowledge is made explicit and can enhance the knowledge depository.

> **KEY CONCEPT**
>
> Data + meaning = information.
> Information + intelligence = knowledge.
> Knowledge + imagination = innovation.

Knowledge creation, which is the foundation of innovation, can be brought about, as we saw in Chapter 4, by the process of socialisation (transformation of knowledge from tacit to tacit), externalisation (transformation of knowledge from tacit to explicit, combination (transformation from explicit to explicit) and internalisation (transformation from explicit to tacit).

Characteristics of an innovative organisation

- Flexible and tolerant culture.
- Trust.
- Believes in knowledge creation and knowledge sharing.
- Provides resources for experimentation.
- Empowers people to implement ideas.
- Recruits people with different backgrounds and interests and with a passion for change.
- Makes every effort to retain talent.
- Creates a physical environment to transfer knowledge.

Case study: the original innovation factory

Thomas Edison cultivated his image as inventor-hero and lone genius, but his greatest creation may have been the invention factory itself. His Menlo Park, New Jersey, laboratory – the

> **KEY CONCEPT**
>
> Incubators for start-up firms are also invention factories – they just invent business models, not physical products.

CONTINUED ... Case study: the original innovation factory

world's first dedicated R & D facility – demonstrated that a stream of promising ideas could be generated if a company was organized in the right way. Rather than focusing on one invention, one field of expertise, or blended elements from past work on telegraphs, telephones and electric motors enabled his inventors to move easily in and out of separate pools of knowledge, to keep learning new ideas, and to use new ideas in novel situations.

A hallmark of Edison's inventions was that they used old ideas, materials, or objects in new ways. The phonograph blended elements from past work on telegraphs, telephones, and electric motors. And the lab's early work on telegraph cables later helped its engineers transform the telephone from a scratchy-sounding novelty into a commercial success. Edison built the laboratory for the 'rapid and cheap development of an invention' and delivered on his promise of a 'minor invention every ten days and a big thing every six months or so.' In his six years of operation, it generated more than 400 patents.

Modern invention factories are springing up everywhere today. Since its founding in 1978 IDEO has developed thousands of products – from the Palm V for 3 Com to the Twist'n Go cup for Pepsi – in more than 40 industries. IDEO's work with companies in dissimilar fields such as medical instruments, furniture, toys, and computers gives the company a broad view of the latest technologies. Lessons from IDEO's diverse client base inspire many original designs. For example, a Chatty Kathy Doll supplied the idea for a reliable inexpensive motor used in a docking station for an Apple laptop computer.

CONTINUED . . . Case study: the original innovation factory

Incubators for start-up firms are also invention factories – they just invent business models, not physical products. Bill Gross's Ideallab! is the most renowned of these. His 'Internet factory' in Pasadena, California, houses about 20 start-ups at any given time. The companies try to succeed on the Internet by entering diverse markets using a broad range of business models. Gross encourages 'cross-pollination' among all the people in the building and is himself a skilled knowledge broker, spreading ideas from one group to another.

Source: Reprinted by permission of *Harvard Business Review*. From 'Building an innovation factory' by Andrew Hargadon and Robert I. Sutton, May–June 2000, p. 157. Copyright © 2000 by the President and Fellows of Harvard College; all rights reserved.

Incubators and innovation

Incubators are formed by specialised organisations and also within other organisations to enable their staff to experiment with ideas and come up with new products/services, process or business models. Incubators hand-hold new entrepreneurial businesses through all of the critical steps of launching and managing new ventures.

Guidelines for establishing incubators

- Be very clear as to the objectives of forming the incubator.
- The members of teams working in an incubator should be committed, passionate and open in their communication.

- Select people with entrepreneurial characteristics to work in incubators.
- Allow them to experiment and make mistakes.
- Provide adequate resources.
- The team should be well briefed on what is required.
- Conduct external benchmarking.
- Establish a time limit for coming up with some results.

Emulating Silicon Valley culture

It is reported that over 5000 businesses are launched every year in Silicon Valley, California. Venture capitalists are eager to finance such start-ups. The Valley has a very high density of companies, all clustered around one another. This means that there is a good pool of talent and there is an appropriate infrastructure for sharing knowledge. Talent is rewarded well and the culture is tolerant to making mistakes and experimenting. The whole environment in the Valley enthuses Netpreneurs. Creating a similar climate elsewhere will foster innovation not only in different countries but also in 'bricks-and-mortar' organisations.

Don't do that!

In her book *The Change Masters*, Rosabeth Moss Kanter highlights the ten rules for *stifling* innovation.[27] These are:

1 Regard any new idea from below with suspicion – because it is new and because it is from below.

2 Insist that people who need your approval to act first go through several other levels of management to get their signatures.

3 Ask departments or individuals to challenge and criticise each other's proposals.

4 Express your criticisms freely and withhold your praise.

5 Treat identification of problems as signs of failure, to discourage people from telling you when something in their area is not working.

6 Control everything very carefully. Make sure people count anything that can be counted frequently.

7 Make decisions to reorganise or change policies in secret and spring them on people unexpectedly.

8 Make sure that requests for information are fully justified and make sure that it is not given out to managers freely. You do not want data to fall into the wrong hands.

9 Assign to lower-level managers, in the name of delegation and participation, responsibility for figuring out how to cut back, lay off, move people around, or otherwise implement threatening decisions you have made – and get them to do it quickly.

10 Above all, never forget that you, the higher-ups, already know everything important about this business.

Even though her book was written in 1984, these rules are still practised today by some of the organisations who are trying to play 'catch-up' by transforming their organisation from 'bricks' to 'clicks'.

How to inspire innovation

Strategy guru Guy Hamel, writing in *Fortune* magazine, highlights ten rules for designing a culture that *inspires* innovation. The article starts:

> Watch a flock of geese turning and swooping in fight. There is no grand vizier goose, no chairman of the gaggle. The geese can't call ahead for a weather report. They can't predict what obstacles they will meet. Yet their course is true. And they are a flock. Complexity theorists describe this as an order without careful crafting, or order for free. The intricate play of the many markets that make up the

global economy, the vibrant diversity of the Internet, the behavior of a colony of ants, that winged arrow of geese – these are just a few instances in which order seems to emerge in an absence of any central authority. All of them have something to teach us about how revolutionary strategies should emerge in a chaotic and ever-changing world. By creating the right set of conditions, one can provoke the emergence of highly ordered things – maybe even such things as revolutionary business concepts . . . This does not mean that top management is irrelevant . . . Its job is to build an organisation that can continually spawn cool new business concepts, to design context rather than invent content. Top management puts into operation rules that can create a deeply innovative organisation – rules like these ten, which helped the likes of Enron, Charles Schwab, GE Capital, and Royal Dutch/Shell become gray-haired revolutionaries, capable of reinventing themselves and their industries again and again.[28]

Hamel's ten rules

1 *Set unreasonable expectations.* This involves setting 'stretch' goals for your business. Without such goals, aspiration loses its credibility.

2 *Stretch your business definition.* Define your business in terms of your strategic assets and your competencies rather than what you do.

3 *Create a cause, not a business.* Unlearning and learning take place if there is a belief in a cause. The cause could be migrating to the Web to provide your customers with what they want, how they want it.

4 *Listen to new voices.* Listen to your employees, your customers and your partners. Promote diversity of thinking.

5 *Design an open market for ideas.* Create an environment where ideas can be communicated freely and avoid prejudices about who is capable of coming up with successful ideas.

6 *Offer an open market for capital.* Accessibility to capital with minimum hurdles is an important factor.

7 *Open up the market for talent.* Create an opportunity for your people to work on different projects and make your talent mobile.

8 *Lower the risks of experimentation.* Start with ideas about small businesses – make a lot of small bets.

9 *Make like a cell – divide and divide.* When companies stop dividing and differentiating, innovation dies.

10 *Pay your innovators well* – really well.

Transforming 'bricks' organisations into 'clicks' organisations

In five years' time, all companies will be internet companies . . . or they won't be companies. (Larry Ellison, CEO of Oracle)

Where does the Internet rank in my business priorities? . . . it's number 1, 2, 3, and 4. (Jack Welch, Chairman of General Electric)

In order to take advantage of the new economy and the Internet, established businesses are transforming themselves and are creating new ways of doing business. *Business 2.0* (June 2000) reported the following story about General Motors:

General Motors Corp. has been known for blowing leads in the market place, but its early efforts on the Net may put the car manufacturer – still the world's largest industrial concern – on the road back to heavy industry leadership on the Net.

Detroit-based GM is aggressively moving every thing it can to Internet-based platforms; from purchasing to manufacturing, marketing to selling. The high-potential

new service OnStar will become a rolling Internet portal in about a million GM vehicles this year.
Hitting hard in e-commerce may be the company's last big chance to return to former glory, tarnished over the last couple of decades. GM's U.S. market share slid steadily, to below 30 per cent, due to some legendary miscalculations, not only regarding the incursions of Japanese auto makers, but also marketing blitzes of cross-town rivals Ford Motor Co. and DaimlerChrysler AG.

Ford Motor Co. has also started doing business on the Internet. The company convinced itself that the Net will reinvent the auto industry. It is now using the Internet to bring bureaucratic layers down and unleash radically new ways of planning, making and selling cars. Ford is striving to be the model of efficiency in the Internet age.

The Internet is prompting organisational transformation and innovation in order to participate in the new economy. If companies do not take advantage of the Net they will no longer be able to compete with e-businesses constituting the new economy.

> **KEY CONCEPT**
>
> The Internet is prompting organisational transform-ation and innovation in order to participate in the new economy.

According to an interview report prepared by Michael Skapinker:

In a garage somewhere, Gary Hamel is fond of saying, an entrepreneur is forging a bullet with your company's name on it. If you lead a large company with a history stretching back decades, chances are some small start-up is going to relegate you to the third division, if not to extinction. Hamel compares the ideas being generated in Silicon Valley today to the creativity and genius of Renaissance Florence. The wealth being created by small Silicon Valley outfits beats that being achieved by large companies.

There were about 90 flotations of Silicon Valley companies last year, Hamel says. The current market capitalisation of those companies is around $245 bn. There are about a million people working in Silicon Valley. That means the area has created $245,000 of new wealth per worker in a single year. Which cluster of 'old economy' companies comes close?

Yet it doesn't have to be this way, Hamel argues. The old economy's decline is not pre-ordained. 'A lot of dot.coms have had a free run over the last few years because large companies just haven't been able to respond quickly enough,' he says.[29]

Innovation and business transformation

Irrespective of the nature of the business, to bring innovation at an organisational level and transform the way business is done attention has to be paid to 7 Ss. These are:

- *Strategy* – analysis of environment, competition, customer needs and the organisation's strengths and weaknesses, leading to a plan or course of action that determines the allocations of the firm's scarce resources, over time, to reach identified goals.
- *Structure* – salient features of the organisation chart, or a description of how the separate entities of an organisation are tied together; formats of status and control.
- *Systems* – procedural reports and routine processes. On the intangible side, this includes routine processes such as meeting formats for conflict management.
- *Staff* – characterisations of major groupings of people within the firm.
- *Style* – description of behavioural patterns or common traits of key managers and the organisation as a whole.
- *Shared values* – the significant meanings or central beliefs that an organisation embeds in its members.
- *Skills* – the one or two distinctive capabilities of the organisation that authentically differentiate it from the competition.

These seven dimensions of business influence its effectiveness. In bringing about organisational transformation, all seven dimensions are affected. However, changes in one or some of these dimensions will not bring about organisational transformation or organisational innovation, which requires a completely different way of doing business. This message is important for 'bricks-and-mortar' organisations wanting to compete in the new economy.

The Internet, knowledge and innovation

The above snapshots indicate the power of the Internet in bringing about organisational and operational innovation. The Internet has also provided an extremely challenging environment for flexible product development. Product designers can continuously refine and shape products even once they are on the market. They can get customer feedback and incorporate that knowledge into product design.

The Internet has facilitated the capture of information, which can be converted into knowledge and this knowledge can be used to bring about innovation and organisational transformation.

Innovation and e-business

An innovative mindset is important for e-business because:

- An e-business operates in a fast-changing world.
- It has to create a new business model – an innovative way of doing business.
- It has to have a web-like structure for its value and supply chain systems.
- These systems have to be configured continuously and in some cases dramatically.

- The focus of strategy is *speed* and an innovative way of gaining and retaining customers.
- It has to use knowledge as a main driver of its business operations, processes and systems.
- It has to deal with individuals with passion, imagination and talent.
- It has to have a 'breakthrough' strategy and mindset.
- Trust is important.

An innovation culture therefore has to be embedded in an e-business for it to gain and sustain competitive advantage.

The Internet and an intranet can play key roles in gathering information, sharing information and converting information into knowledge, providing speed and economies of cost.

Knowledge management strategy and innovation

There are three distinct strategies that organisations adopt in relation to managing knowledge, affecting innovation and the innovation process within the organisation.[30] These strategies are:

- Codification.
- Personalisation.
- A mixture of the two.

Codification

Many organisations have put systems in place to codify, store and reuse knowledge. A codification strategy takes a people-to-document approach.

Let us assume that an organisation is involved in an outsourcing project. The main objective of the project is to prospect for a new partner and then to negotiate and establish a deal with that partner.

Once the deal is completed the people involved will undertake a review and record their experience in terms of processes involved, experience gained, obstacles to be overcome and the way the project was managed. They will also record who was involved and their competencies.

Once this knowledge is codified it can be accessed by any individual in the organisation and the knowledge can be reused, thus stopping reinventing the wheel.

For a codification strategy to work properly, the organisation has to have a knowledge-sharing culture and systems to help knowledge workers contribute to this culture. Systems have to be developed that codify, store and disseminate knowledge. In some businesses specialist personnel are employed to help codify the knowledge and form and enhance the corporate knowledge memory.

A codification strategy does not exclude face-to-face meetings or conversations in whatever format. The focus of knowledge formation and sharing is on the codifying process.

Personalisation

This strategy emphasises dialogue between individuals. Knowledge is shared by individuals in meetings, brainstorming sessions, one-to-one conversations and sharing knowledge across the floor. In this way tacit knowledge is shared among individuals.

This type of strategy does not exclude codification. Refererence could be made to knowledge maps or to knowledge directory contacts with individuals who have tacit knowledge of specialised projects. Such information facilitates making direct contact via telephone or video conferencing to the source of knowledge.

Individuals under this strategy develop networks of people. The organisation also encourages formation of networks by getting individuals with different expertise and locations to work on projects together and thus consolidate the practice of networking.

A mixture of the two approaches

Rather than focusing on one approach and using the other approach as a support, some organisations pay equal attention to both approaches, codification and personalisation.

Which strategy to adopt?

The strategic approach an organisation should adopt depends on the nature of its business. If a business deals with similar problems again and again, the codification approach is appropriate because it allows reuse of knowledge and also the speed of getting this knowledge will reduce the cost and enhance revenue. In fact, such a strategy can also reduce cost of providing solutions to customers.

Dell Computer, by the very nature of its business, does not deal with highly customised orders. The company adopts a codification strategy that is consistent with its business model. Knowledge reuse is the main driver of Dell's business.

IBM, on the other hand, adopts a personalisation approach, which is consistent with its strategy. The company encourages person-to-person exchanges to come up with innovative products in order to compete with competitors effectively.

Innovation in products and processes requires knowledge sharing, mainly tacit knowledge. In this situation the personalisation approach is more appropriate.

In an e-business, because of constant change and constant review of its business model, the personalisation approach will be appropriate. However, if it has to provide a standardised product, it has to think adopting codification strategy to take advantage of the economies of reuse.

> **KEY CONCEPT**
>
> E-businesses operate in a turbulent and complex environment. Such an environment necessitates moving decision making to the coal face (hence empowerment).

The personalisation approach is appropriate for a business dealing with high customisation.

E-businesses operate in a turbulent and complex environment. Such an environment necessitates moving decision making to the coal face (hence empowerment). In a climate like this, an e-business has to innovate constantly and make sure, as much as possible, that its competitors do not imitate it. This is one of the ways of sustaining competitive advantage over time.

The more tacit knowledge an organisation has and uses, the more difficult it is to imitate. Some strategists have argued that competitive advantage can only be sustained if the capabilities creating the advantage are supported by resources that are not easily imitated. Knowledge is difficult to imitate and tacit knowledge is even more so. Tacit knowledge is skill and experience based and constitutes the organisation's intangible asset.

However, the late Akin Morita of Sony said that imitation is inevitable in the long run. Innovative companies can dominate the market for a year or so, but gradually the imitators will enter the market, possibly within months, as the track record of innovative companies becomes established.

Stopping imitation involves various mechanisms, some of which involve resorting to legal protection in the form of intellectual property rights, that is, knowledge embedded in documents, products, designs and processes. This is explored in Chapter 10.

Key messages

◆ Innovation is important for any business. It has to be part of its survival strategy.

◆ Innovation is particularly important for an e-business if it is to be responsive to external changes.

◆ Innovation depends on knowledge creation and transfer within an organisation. Without knowledge there is no innovation.

◆ The relationship between innovation and knowledge is a two-way relationship. Knowledge creates innovation, which in turn creates new knowledge.

◆ Organisations have to have an appropriate culture, structure and systems to foster innovation.

◆ Incubators are springing up to nurture start-ups and foster innovation. These incubators are independent of organisations, though some companies form incubators within the organisation to retain talent.

◆ Beware of stifling innovation.

◆ Britain is on track for digital business and innovation.

◆ Innovation is related to the type of knowledge management strategy that the organisation adopts.

◆ An e-business has to monitor external changes constantly and be in a position – strategically, structurally and conceptually – to respond to these changes.

The learning organisation

CHAPTER 9

The manager of the future will simply be a learning guide.
(Peter Drucker)

Overview

To create knowledge, organisations have to become learning organisations. To do so involves acquiring new skills of learning and overcoming various barriers to learning.

The learning organisation is an appropriate mode for an e-business, which has to use knowledge to compete successfully.

There has to be a different type of leadership and this leadership has to provide a climate for learning.

The Internet can be used effectively to transform a business into a learning organisation.

The knowledge-driven organisation must necessarily be a learning organisation. The guru of the learning organisation is Peter Senge, director of the Systems Thinking and Organisational Learning Program at the Sloan School of Management, MIT. According to him, learning organisations are places 'where people continually expand their capacity to create results they truly desire, where new and expansive patterns of thinking are nurtured, where collective aspirations is set free, and where people are continually learning how to learn together'.

The attributes of a learning organisation

- The concept of the learning organisation is a vision.
- The learning organisation has to continually expand its capacity to be creative and innovative.
- Learning has to be part of the culture.
- It acquires knowledge and leverages it by learning.
- It has intellectual (thinking) and pragmatic (doing) dimensions.
- It oozes with enthusiasm, energy and commitment.
- It fosters the development of people.
- It has open communication.

> **KEY CONCEPT**
>
> Learning has to be part of the organisational culture.

E-business and the learning organisation

An e-business has to do the following:

- Come up with a new business model and a web-like value chain.
- Leverage knowledge to constantly configure its business to respond to a complex environment that is changing all the time.
- Manage and nurture talent.
- Use the Internet to expand its capacity to innovate.
- Empower its people.
- Have free and open communication.

> **KEY CONCEPT**
>
> An e-business, by necessity, has to be a learning organisation.

Technology can give organisations success in a wider market, but they must first learn to understand the dynamics of dealing with customers via the Internet and the value of collaboration. The e-business has one advantage in that it does not have to unlearn old habits, as do established businesses.

Learning to collaborate has become the name of the game especially in the field of business-to-business (B2B) commerce. Covisint, for example, a joint trading exchange, is supported by General Motors, Ford, DaimlerChrysler, Renault and Nissan.

Infobank is another example of an organisation that has learnt to transform itself and formed an electronic commerce division in 1993. According to the *Sunday Times* (3 December 2000):

> Infobank quickly realised that many companies were keen to set up their own trading exchanges but were unsure how to go about it. It decided that the way forward was a 'one-box' solution and created the e-hub software, which is basically an exchange in a single piece of software.

This is a good example of how an organisation can pick up clues in the changing external environment and come up with an innovative business model to gain competitive advantage. According to *The Economist* (18 November 2000):

> Managing collaboration requires special skills: less emphasis on individual achievement, more on teamwork. Moreover, just as companies can learn lessons from developing online HR services for their own staff that can be applied to running online support for their customers, so the lessons they learn from collaborating within the organisations can be applied to collaboration with other companies.

PAUSE FOR THOUGHT: Failure to learn

Tom Stewart (*Business Week*, 27 November 2000) highlights the fact that even an organisation like Ford, which is a knowledge-based organisation, sometimes fails to learn and creates a business fiasco. Stewart writes:

> Ford and Firestone are suffering the death of 1,000 cuts in part because of catastrophic failure to share knowledge. Information that might have alerted the companies to the calamitous mismatch of Ford Explorers and Firestone tires was scattered in different places in both companies, each item innocuous in isolation. The irony: If Jacques Nasser wants to make sure such a failure never happens again, he'll find one of the most successful, tried-and-proven schemes for knowledge sharing at his own company. Ford's Best Practices Replication Process has produced a billion-dollar benefit for the automaker. An interesting question is why it didn't help in this case.

The simple answer is that there has been a failure in sharing knowledge. However, a learning organisation has to anticipate such situations and use its knowledge to be proactive. A knowledge-based organisation also has to be a learning organisation in order to minimise or even eliminate such business failures.

Types of learning

There are various different types of learning, including the following.

Maintenance learning

In this type of learning organisations discover better ways of doing what they have been doing. Maintenance learning does not question the organisation's strategy or its way of doing business. If an organisation has a shortage of staff it decides to go out there and recruit more people rather than look at radical ways to see if it can achieve 'strategic stretch' of its existing competencies.

An organisation with only maintenance learning capacity and process will lack the capability to use intellectual capital effectively and it will fail to involve its people in creating the alternative futures so crucial for the e-business environment.

Anticipatory learning

This mode of learning involves questioning all the assumptions on which businesses view the future. Formulating strategy, for example, in an e-business is *planning to anticipate surprises*. Scenario planning involves putting processes into place for anticipatory learning. Knowledge-driven organisations have to be involved in anticipatory learning in order to be adaptive to changing situations. Anticipatory learning prepares organisations to deal with future environments and complexity.

> **KEY CONCEPT**
>
> An e-business must build the capacity for anticipatory learning.

Generative learning

This type of learning reflects the distinction between what is called 'single-loop' and 'double-loop' learning.

Single-loop learning

This prepares organisations to be reactive – whenever you have a skill shortage you recruit more talent; whenever revenues fall you increase promotional spending, for example.

Single-loop learning occurs when organisations face problems and mistakes. They make attempts to deal with

problems without changing the fundamentals of doing
business.

A thermostat, as an example, is capable of single-loop
learning. If the temperature goes too high or too low, it will
respond to bring it back to a set level. It does not, however,
determine what an ideal temperature should be. It does not
analyse and question the causes that create variations.

Double-loop learning

This enables organisations to resolve problems but in doing
so question the strategy and the fundamentals of doing
business and also the values of the organisation. The benefit
of double-loop learning is increased effectiveness in decision
making and an acceptance of failures and mistakes, the
conditions necessary for the learning organisation.

Double-loop learning is generative
learning. It leads to the creation of
new business models consistent with a
complex and changing environment.
E-business itself, with its distinct
value chain, is the result of the process
of double-loop learning. Innovation is
also the result of double-loop learning.

> **KEY CONCEPT**
>
> The success of an
> e-business depends on
> double-loop learning.

Furthermore, the learning organisation should incorporate an
inclusive learning process, providing opportunities to learn for
all its employees, and *reflective learning*, which embraces the
capacity to learn *how* to learn. The development of reflective
learning will enhance knowledge creation and sustain
competitive advantage.

A strategy to promote learning on its own is not enough for
its success. It must be accompanied by a knowledge management strategy that addresses the issues of knowledge creation,
the process of knowledge creation, knowledge transfer and the
use of knowledge to gain competitive advantage.

Learning styles

A number of learning styles have been identified and studied over the years by many psychologists and other experts. For example, Kolb proposes a theory of experiential learning that involves four principal stages in the process of learning.[31] They are:

- Concrete experience.
- Reflective observation.
- Abstract conceptualisation.
- Active experimentation.

Concrete material provides the raw material for reflective observation, which can lead to the formulation of concepts, which may be tested in new situations.

According to Kolb, different people develop particular learning styles because they use one of these stages more than others. As a result, four types of learners develop: activists, reflectors, theorists and pragmatists. All these types of learners are important in a business environment consisting of various operational dimensions.

The learning organisation needs all these types of learners.

Learning and knowledge formation

As we saw in Chapter 4, Nonaka presented four modes of knowledge transformation, socialisation, externalisation, combination and internalisation. In practice it is difficult to divorce learning from knowledge creation and his model is applicable to the learning organisation.

Socialisation transforms tacit knowledge into more tacit knowledge. In this mode individuals share their learning, which they have acquired by experience and observation. If this learning is not shared then no knowledge is created.

It is important to note that what is transferred is not information but experience, with the associated emotions and context.

Externalisation, transforms tacit knowledge into explicit knowledge. If a person has learned how to manage the complexity of the business environment and as a consequence prepares a model of a value chain appropriate for that business environment, they are putting their learning into practice and articulating their tacit knowledge so that it becomes explicit knowledge.

The team examining such a model gets involved in a reflective learning process. In Sillicon Valley many individuals involved in start-ups operate in an externalisation mode of knowledge creation.

Combination is when explicit knowledge is transformed into more explicit knowledge. In the above example, the configuration of the new value chain has become explicit. When this configuration is embedded in systems and processes, it is made explicit. Individuals operating such a system learn from embedded knowledge and create their own experience in the process.

Internalisation transforms knowledge from explicit to tacit. In the above example individuals work within the value chain of the business and acquire their own experience through the process of inclusive learning. This experience is internalised and becomes part of the individual. Each now has tacit knowledge of this new process.

Relationship between learning, knowledge, the value chain and customers

Learning takes place by individuals. It is transformed into organisational learning by exchanging information and experiences. When information is put into context it becomes knowledge, which is then embedded in products, service and processes, assuming that the organisation has a strategy of knowledge management. Embedded knowledge creates value, which is transferred to customers. Customers should be encouraged to provide feedback on their own value propositions and the extent to which the value added by the organisation meet their values. Such feedback should be learned and information transferred to the organisation. This information creates new knowledge.

Learning, knowledge creation, value-adding processes in value chain, customer satisfaction, retention and loyalty are thus all inter-related.

Barriers to the learning organisation

Organisations find it difficult to unlearn. This is one of the challenges facing 'bricks' organisations in transforming themselves into 'clicks' organisations. Some like to maintain the status quo – if ain't broke, don't fix it.

Learning and unlearning have to take place at people level. One of the key factors inhibiting learning in an established business as opposed to a start-up is that some employees have gone through a climate of delayering, restructuring, down-sizing and cost cutting. Business process reengineering also took a tremendous toll on people. Some organisations, in responding to various management initiatives, have caught a potentially lethal disease called 'corporate anorexia'. Such a disease manifests itself in two ways:

● The organisation has lost the ability to be creative, which is very important for operating in the new economy.

● Employees work in a climate of uncertainty and hence find it difficult to give their best and help their organisation become a learning organisation.

Employees in such organisations are also suffering from 'initiative fatigue'.

However, the business landscape is changing dramatically. The Internet is altering the nature of business, the nature of competition and the nature of customers. Unless organisations are prepared to become learning organisations and do so fast, they will not be able to use knowledge to gain competitive advantage and their survival will be short-lived.

In practice, it is not easy to become a learning organisation. Various barriers exist in relation to culture, strategy, structure, system and competencies.

Key barriers include the following:

- The organisational structure creates barriers to free and open communication.
- It does not know how to manage people.
- It does not understand the importance of intangible assets.
- It does not have a knowledge management strategy in place.
- Its systems and culture stifle innovation.
- There is no staff development training.
- There is no incentive to retain talent.

The learning organisation has to be an adaptive organisation. It has to be willing and committed to benchmark against best practice. A tolerant and collaborative culture is important. In his book *The Fifth Discipline*,[32] Peter Senge gives the example of the founder of Polaroid. The inventor of instant photography had a plaque on his office wall that read, 'A mistake is an event the full benefit of which has not yet been turned to your advantage.'

IMPLEMENTATION CHECKLIST: key success factors for becoming the learning organisation

1 Continuously monitor the external environment.
2 Capture information.
3 Benchmark to adopt best practice.
4 Learn from your partners.
5 Institute changes.
6 Communicate, communicate and communicate.
7 Build and manage knowledge.
8 Recruit and retain talent.
9 Empower your employees.
10 Do not take your eyes off your customers.

Why has learning become important?

We now operate within the context of the new economy where knowledge becomes one of the key drivers to superior business performance. Businesses have to add value through knowledge, just-in-time systems, real-time decision making, innovation and building networks of partnerships. This they do by using the Internet.

Customers, in return, use the Internet to access information on products and services, thus learning and building knowledge that they leverage to satisfy their needs. Businesses, if they are to be successful, have to be one step ahead of the customers. To do so is to become a learning organisation.

> **KEY CONCEPT**
>
> An e-business has to be skilled at creating, acquiring and transferring knowledge, and at modifying its behaviour to reflect new knowledge and insights. This is what the learning organisation is all about.

An e-business has to be skilled at creating, acquiring and transferring knowledge, and at modifying its behaviour to reflect new knowledge and insights. This is what the learning organisation is all about.

How to become a learning organisation

According to Peter Senge, there are five essential disciplines for a learning organisation:

- Personal mastery.
- Mental models.
- Shared vision.
- Team learning.
- Systems thinking.

Personal mastery

Personal mastery is focused on individuals. It is *individuals* in the organisation who learn, create knowledge and transform knowledge into collective and organisational knowledge. Organisations simply provide an environment for learning and knowledge creation.

Without individuals there is no learning, no knowledge and no innovation. This is why it is important to recruit and retain people whose values are congruent with organisational values.

Personal mastery is about individual growth and learning. According to Senge:

> Personal mastery goes beyond competence and skills, though it is grounded in competence and skills. It goes beyond spiritual unfolding or opening, although it requires spiritual growth. It means approaching one's life as a creative work, living life from a creative as opposed to reactive viewpoint.

Components of personal mastery include individuals' values, continuously asking and clarifying what is important and learning to see current reality more clearly. Learning in this context does not mean simply collecting more information, but truly converting knowledge to bring about desired results.

> **KEY CONCEPT**
>
> Personal mastery is about continuously developing yourself – it is a process or a journey, not a destination.

This discipline is difficult to understand for people in western cultures and for hard-nosed business people. Nevertheless, personal mastery is very important for knowledge workers who have different values and aspirations and want an opportunity to examine themselves.

Personal development is not just about learning interpersonal communication skills or assertiveness techniques or understanding the mechanics of knowledge creation and management. It is about total development of yourself.

Mental models

Each individual has an 'internal' image of the world based on certain assumptions. Individual behaviour is guided by these mental models, which are the result of our experience, education and environment.

> **KEY CONCEPT**
>
> We can become prisoners of our own thinking.

Mental models can and do constitute barriers to knowledge creation and learning. If we perceive that the organisation we work for really does not care for us, does not appreciate us or is unfair in its dealings, we will act accordingly by not making an effective contribution to that organisation. We will not be an active participant in the knowledge creation and transfer process. We will resist change and we will not learn on behalf of the organisation.

For an e-business to be successful, it needs agility, and for that it has to empower its employees. Trust in employees has to be transparent and employees have to feel trusted, otherwise they will not enable the business to achieve its strategic objectives. They have to perceive that their organisation really values their efforts and contribution.

Mental models affect us in the way we deal with our colleagues and partners. In a web-based organisation such as an e-business, we require positive mental models in order to form trustworthy and collaborative partnerships and networks.

Mental models also affect the way we make decisions. In the past we have been trained to make decisions based on linear thinking, proceeding stage by stage to arrive at a solution. In the new economy, employees have to be trained to be lateral thinkers and decisions are based on shared understanding of inter-relationships and complexity.

Shared vision

Shared vision incorporates the involvement of many individuals. Everyone in the organisation has to understand the vision of the business and be involved in implementing it. A shared vision gives meaning to work and it prompts

> **KEY CONCEPT**
>
> People working in Silicon Valley get their buzz out of shared vision and the challenges presented to them. Such an attitude creates an innovative spirit – the birth of Netpreneurs.

contribution and effort. It is a good incentive for learning – a way of winning the 'hearts and minds' of employees.

When vision is shared the task becomes part of the self. People working in Silicon Valley get their buzz out of shared vision and the challenges presented to them. Such an attitude creates an innovative spirit – the birth of Netpreneurs.

Team learning

Collective knowledge is created by working in teams. Individuals brainstorm, have conversations, exchange experiences, work on projects in teams. Organisational knowledge results from team learning. At the end of each project or assignment, team members can get together to reflect on their experiences, their competencies, the way they have worked on the projects, what worked and what did not work. Such exchanges promote

> **KEY CONCEPT**
>
> In an e-business, because of networks and partnerships, team learning can be a good resource for the business to capture knowledge and enhance its capability to do business effectively.

individual and team learning and tacit and explicit knowledge. Team learning generates synergy within the organisation.

Team learning is an effective way of understanding cross-functional cultures. In an e-business, because of networks and partnerships, team learning can be a good resource for the business to capture knowledge and enhance its capability to do business effectively.

Systems thinking – the fifth discipline

Systems thinking integrates the other four disciplines and it enables the organisation to see the 'big picture'. Systems thinking is fundamental to any learning organisation. Without systems thinking, each of the other disciplines will be isolated, which will not help generate organisation learning.

Case study: Apple Japan

Until 1989, Apple Japan, the Japanese arm of the multinational Apple Computing Corporation, held only 1 per cent of the country's personal computer market. The appointment of a new company president marked the beginning of an era – he started the drive to increase

CONTINUED ... Case study: Apple Japan

Apple's presence in the market and accelerated change. The company was to achieve annual sales of $1 billion by the end of 1995.

To meet this challenge the corporation approached the management consulting firm Arthur D. Little, which has built up a wealth of experience in information technology and company restructuring. Apple Japan requested a sweeping plan to penetrate the market and increase efficiency within the company. In order to do this, it planned to reposition the brand, expand the range of distributors, improve customer management, and introduce the concept of the learning organisation into the workplace.

Methods

In order to implement learning organisation techniques, Apple was advised to tackle the five disciplines that are essential to a learning organisation: team learning, shared visions, mental models, personal mastery and systems thinking.

Although group meetings were a regular part of company practice, more time was allowed for group discussions and team education. This kept the work teams well informed and increased every individual's input to their project. With the increased emphasis on team learning, a shared vision was naturally introduced, allowing each member to work towards the same goal irrespective of their position.

Each employee of the company had their own mental model of how the organisation, their managers and team colleagues operate. By trying to bring each person's

CONTINUED . . . Case study: Apple Japan

mental model into line with the rest of the team, the learning process was made more efficient and teams acted more coherently. Personal mastery was also addressed by encouraging managers to set their staff challenging but reasonable goals, and introducing training programmes. The crucial discipline was systems thinking, which brought all the other factors together. This enabled each employee to make decisions, taking the whole system into account, instead of focusing specifically on their own problems.

These disciplines were implemented by moderate restructuring and a programme of education that was applied to everyone in the organisation.

Results

The reorganisation resulted in a marked improvement in company sales, with growth exceeding the most optimistic projections:

- Market share grew to 15 per cent in 1995 from 1 per cent in 1989.
- Annual sales soared to $1.3 billion in 1994, with the sale of 520 000 computers.

Although not all of the success can be attributed to the introduction of the learning organisation concept, the results indicate an unprecedented improvement. The learning organisation was a major player in instituting this growth.

Source: Students' project, University of Edinburgh.

Learning in an e-business

By its very nature, an e-business competes according to new rules. It is constantly adapting to the new environment. It therefore has to constantly experiment. Experimenting involves risk. This is what distinguishes 'bricks' businesses

> **KEY CONCEPT**
>
> 'The rate at which organisations learn may become the only sustainable source of competitive advantage.'
> (Peter Senge)

from 'clicks' business. A 'clicks' businesses will experience many failures because it is working within the new economy and it has to experiment and take risks. Failures can be seen as stepping stones towards success.

Managing risks

Risks can be managed in the following ways:

- Benchmarking. This provides information on how other businesses are doing and on best practice.

> **KEY CONCEPT**
>
> Experimenting involves risk. This is what distinguishes 'bricks' businesses from 'clicks' businesses.

- Encouraging knowledge sharing. 'Today's problems come from yesterday's solutions' is one of the laws of *The Fifth Discipline*.
- Employing the right people for the job.
- Retaining talent, thus reducing talent turnover.
- Leveraging knowledge.
- Involving most employees in strategy formulation.
- Open communication.
- Reflecting on successes as well as failures. People generally do not like sharing bad experiences. Disappointments and failures are part of the learning process and the organisation must encourage employees to share such experiences.

- Transferring knowledge quickly and effectively throughout the organisation.
- Monitoring the external and internal environment continuously.
- Forming partnerships and alliances to spread risks and to acquire new knowledge.
- Listening to your customers.
- Installing a feedback system.
- Institutionalising trust.

The role of the Internet in managing risks

The Internet provides:

- An opportunity to network, establishing alliances and creating networks.
- Speed. Decisions can be taken, feedback given and information transferred in real time.
- Cost economies.
- A mechanism for sharing information.
- A way of conducting conversations, which is important for transforming tacit knowledge into explicit knowledge.
- Global reach for learning.
- Accelerated learning.
- Knowledge management throughout the organisation.

Leadership in the learning organisation

As already indicated, leadership in the new economy has to be a matter of substance not style. In relation to the learning organisation, the main role of a leader should be to foster systems thinking. The other

> **KEY CONCEPT**
>
> To play new games requires an understanding of the creation of new rules. The leader should act as a coach and a mentor.

four disciplines have to be co-ordinated, which constitutes the core competence of the organisation. According to Senge, the leader's role in the learning organisation is that of a designer, teacher and steward who can build shared vision and challenge prevailing mental models.

To play new games requires an understanding of the creation of new rules. The leader should act as a coach and a mentor. This point has often been made but it is very important in relation to e-business.

The role of a coach is to bring out the best performance from people and to create an environment where staff give their full commitment and expertise. Coaching in the learning organisation is developmentally based rather than merely task oriented.

A leader in a learning organisation should:

- act as a coach;
- free up information and encourage knowledge creation;
- provide resources to show commitment;
- take part in the learning process;
- get rid of a blame culture;
- reward and recognise your staff and be fair to all;
- facilitate individual development;
- share the vision and involve people in strategy formulation;
- create an 'I'm OK and You're OK' feeling;
- listen for various possibilities.

If you should try to understand me through the eyes of your experience, your only understanding will be mis-understanding.

For we have walked different paths and have known different fears. And that which brings you laughter just might bring me tears.

So if you can learn to accept me and the strange things I say and do, maybe, through your acceptance you will gain understanding. (Anon.)

One of the first organisations to realise the importance of learning and knowledge was IBM, which adopted 'Think' as its motto. Unfortunately, it is not the motto that drives business performance but action. Unless leaders understand their people and their customers and the value of learning and *do* something about it, no motto in the world can deliver superior performance.

Managing creative destruction

The learning organisation has the capability to manage 'creative destruction':

> The modern organisation is a destabiliser. It must be organised for innovation . . . And it must be organised for systematic abandonment of whatever is established, customary, familiar and comfortable . . . In short it must be organised for constant change. The organisation's function is to put knowledge to work – on tools, products, and processes; on the design of work; on knowledge itself. It is the nature of knowledge that it changes fast and that today's uncertainties always become tomorrow's absurdities.[33]

Even though Drucker did not specifically refer to e-business, what he wrote applies more to e-business and those organisations who are transforming themselves to become e-businesses.

 PAUSE FOR THOUGHT

In the new economy it is imperative for organisations to break away from old ways of thinking. Leaders have to make sure that what they hope for and what they reward are consistent. Steven Kerr highlighted the findings of his research in what managers do and what they reward (see Table 9.1).

Table 9.1: Aspirations and rewards

Managers hope for:	But they reward:
Teamwork and collaboration	The best individual performance
Innovative thinking and risk taking	Proven methods and not making mistakes
Development of people skills	Technical achievements and accomplishments
Employee involvement and empowerment	Tight control over operations and resources
High achievement	Another year's routine effort
Commitment to quality	Shipping on time even with defects
Long-term goals	Quarterly earnings

Source: Steven Kerr (1995) 'An Academy Classic: On the Folly of Rewarding A While Hoping for B', *Academy of Management Executive*, 9(1).

Key messages

◆ A learning organisation enhances organisational capabilities to manage complexity and achieve competitive advantage.

◆ A learning organisation is not a process; it is a vision.

◆ It affects strategic thinking and the value of the organisation.

◆ There are different types of learning and different styles of learning.

◆ Anticipatory learning involves transformation of mindsets and it is important for e-businesses.

◆ A distinction should be drawn between single-loop learning and double-loop learning. Single-loop learning is short-term learning and it makes the organisation reactive, while at the same time maintaining the status quo. Double-loop learning, on the other hand, involves questioning the fundamentals of business.

◆ Learning and knowledge are inter-related. This inter-relationship affects the value chain and customer value propositions.

CONTINUED . . . **Key messages**

◆ There are many barriers to becoming a learning organisation. The organisation has to overcome these barriers.

◆ To become a learning organisation, attention should be paid to five disciplines: personal mastery, team learning, shared vision, mental models and systems thinking.

◆ Leadership in the learning organisation has to be transformational and fair.

Intellectual property protection: the legal dimension of knowledge management

Law is the guardian of civilisation and progress. (Anon.)

Overview

Some forms of knowledge, once embedded in products, processes and symbols, can be legally protected to stop its abuse by competitors and others.

Without such protection there will be no incentive for organisations to invest heavily in research and development.

Because an e-business has to deal with different forms of knowledge, embedded and embrained, and because its web-like relationships with its employees, customers and partners involve working on trust, it becomes important to understand the nature of protection.

CONTINUED . . . Overview

The Internet, apart from its attribute of creating knowledge, also enables organisations to 'steal' intellectual property. New forms of intellectual property, such as domain names, have come into existence and the law has to recognise such developments. There is also the question of security on the Internet. The chapter discusses 'encryption' and biometrics.

The internet provides unrestricted use of knowledge and gives the public access to information. However, organisations providing information on the Internet have to protect its use.

Generally, organisations embed knowledge in their products, processes and documents and they are willing to share this knowledge with the public as long as some protection is accorded to this knowledge.

MP3.com, the Internet music website, was ordered to pay at least $118 million (£82 million) in damages to Universal Music after a landmark copyright infringement ruling. (*The Times*, 9 September 2000)

When knowledge is embedded in products, processes and documents, it is transformed into intellectual property. Inventions, trademarks and industrial designs constitute industrial property and they are protected by registration. Copyright, which deals mainly with literary work, photographic and audiovisual works, musical and artistic works, does not have to be registered in order to gain protection.

Organisations and countries create knowledge and this knowledge is transferred and used. But in order to establish a balance between the transfer and use of knowledge in the public arena and protecting investment and providing incentives to organisations to innovate and create new knowledge, laws have to be established to protect intellectual property.

The World Intellectual Property Organisation (WIPO), a specialised agency of the United Nations, is the world body responsible for promoting the protection of intellectual property by means of inter-governmental co-operation. In relation to the protection of intellectual property, WIPO administers:

- The Berne Convention on the Protection of Literary and Artistic Works.
- The Paris Convention on the Protection of Industrial Property.
- The Washington Treaty on Intellectual Property in respect of Integrated Circuits.

In addition, the World Trade Organisation (WTO) administers the Trade-Related Aspects of Intellectual Property Rights, including trade in counterfeit goods (TRIPS). This agreement has three main features:

1 The establishment of minimum substantive standards of protection for each of the main categories of intellectual property rights.
2 The specification of procedures and remedies to be available in national law so that the rights can be effectively enforced.
3 The application of the WTO dispute-settlement mechanism to TRIPS obligations.

The development of the digital economy and the Internet has posed a very big challenge to regulatory authorities at national and international level. The two broad issues relate to how to manage intellectual property rights at international level; and how to police breaches of intellectual property rights.

Digital transmission enhances knowledge transfer and with it the use of intellectual property and dramatic exploitation of work across national boundaries. Before examining how regulatory authorities meet such a challenge, it is useful to explore various mechanisms by which intellectual property rights can be protected.

All legal protection mechanisms aim to achieve the following:

- Protection of research and development investment.
- Safeguards on return on such investment.
- Facilitation of transfer of knowledge within the legal framework. Licensing to use the technology is an example.
- Generally speaking, the law does not protect ideas as such, but rather ideas transformed into specific forms.

Types of protection

Patents

Patents protect inventions for processes, machines and products. Most computer software-related inventions are either processes or machines. An inventor can apply for a patent in order to stop others copying their invention.

Requirements for applying for a patent
- The invention must be new.
- It must involve an inventory step which in law is defined as 'not obvious to a person skilled in the relevant art'.
- It must be capable of industrial application.
- It must not fall into one of the excepted categories.

The inventor or the organisation for which the invention was conducted can apply for a patent. In order to determine whether the invention is new, research has to be conducted by the Patent Office.

If the invention has been made by a person in the course of employment, the employer is entitled to claim the patent. In all other cases the patent belongs to the inventor.

A patent is granted initially for four years, renewable at four-yearly intervals up to a maximum of 20 years. Fees have to be paid at each stage of renewal.

The patentee has the right to deal in the patent once registered and they can also license others to use the invention exclusively.

In practice, once a patent is published competitors will try to design a product very similar to one patented without infringing patent law. A patent grants its

> **KEY CONCEPT**
>
> Always mark your product with its patent number.

owner the exclusive right to make, use and sell the invention.

If a patent is infringed the remedies will be:

- Injunction – a court order restraining the infrginer from continued sales.
- Damages.
- Destruction of infringement articles.
- A declaration that the patent has been infringed.

Infringement damages can in some cases be avoided if the plaintiff failed to mark the product with its patent number.

Design rights

If a design has 'eye appeal' it can be the subject of registration. However, the copyright, designs and patents law created a system of design protection irrespective of 'eye appeal'.

A design can be registered if:

■ It relates to features of shape, configuration, pattern or ornament.
■ It is new.
■ The features have 'eye appeal'.
■ The features are applied to articles by an industrial process.

The protection is granted for five years, renewable at five-yearly intervals up to a maximum of 25 years. Unregistered designs are protected by copyright, designs and patents law. This protection does not require designs to:

■ be registered;
■ have 'eye appeal';

The period of protection is shorter than that for registered designs.

The main advantage of registered designs over an unregistered design right is that the latter can only be used to prevent copying, whereas a registered design is a true monopoly and applies even if the alleged infringer honestly came up with the same or a similar design independently and without copying.

Trade secrets

Trade secrets protection arises from common law or state statutes. Although strictly speaking not part of intellectual property, the protection is necessary, especially for start-ups trying to discuss their projects with venture capitalists, bankers or other potential financiers.

An obligation of confidence may be expressed in a contract or implied by the circumstances. Trade secrets rights are limited to prevention of copying and cannot be used to prevent another's independent development of the protected information.

E-business, for example, exists on partnerships and in the process of developing a network confidential information may come into existence.

Trademarks

A trademark may be a picture, a word, a sound, a colour or a symbol. The law defines trademarks as 'any sign capable of being represented graphically which is capable of distinguishing goods or services'.

Requirements of registration

The trademark must be:

- Distinctive.
- Capable of graphic presentation.
- Intended for use in the course of trade.

The trademark is recognised by registration in respect of specific goods or services.

If the trademark is being used and the same or a similar mark starts to be used by a competitor, there are two ways to stop the competitor. First, it is possible to sue under common law to restrain the 'passing off'. To succeed in such an action the onus would be to prove the following:

- The plaintiff had a reputation in your name.
- The public would be confused by the competitor's actions.
- The plaintiff has suffered or is likely to suffer damage as a consequence.

Secondly, action can be taken for infringement of a registered mark. Infringements can include if a competitor is using:

- an identical mark on identical goods;
- a similar mark on identical goods;
- an identical mark on similar goods;
- a similar mark on similar goods.

Copyright

As the name implies, this is the right to prevent someone from copying your work. There is no copyright in ideas, only the particular form in which the idea is represented.

Under UK law, copyright subsists in:

- Original literary, dramatic, musical and artistic works.
- Sound recordings, films, broadcasts and cable programmes.

One of the most popular means of protection for computer software is copyright law.

The period of protection for copyright is long compared with patents or registered designs. In most cases the protection is related to the life of the author plus 50 or 70 years. There is no registration.

> **KEY CONCEPT**
>
> Intellectual property reflects the ingenuity and creativity of humanity.

For sound recordings, broadcasts and cable programmes, the period of protection is 50 years from the end of the year in which the work was released.

Intellectual assets

Intellectual assets are becoming increasingly important in the new economy. As we have seen, they come into existence as a result of knowledge being embedded in products and processes and knowledge embodied in people and reflected in the works produced.

For such activities to take place and for knowledge to be transferred for the benefit of customers, employees, partners and the community in general, it is important to be aware of the existence of such protection. Regulatory and legal frameworks also facilitate the creation of more intellectual assets that are essential for the promotion of business, including e-businesses operating in the new economy. Such assets include reputation of business, manufacturing process, design and innovation.

 PAUSE FOR THOUGHT: Discovering new value in intellectual property

Richard Thoman is not your typical chief executive officer. Most Fortune 500 CEOs, when asked how they intend to increase shareholder value, will talk about increasing sales, creating new leading-edge product lines, or pursuing mergers and acquisitions. But Thoman, who was appointed CEO of the $20 billion Xerox Corporation last summer, isn't content with such conventional strategies. He believes one of the strategic keys to Xerox's future is something so intangible, so invisible to traditional bottom-line thinking and corporate practice, that it doesn't even show up on the balance sheet.

'My focus is intellectual property,' he declares. 'I am convinced that the management of intellectual property is how value added is going to be created at Xerox. And not just here, either. Increasingly, companies that are good at managing IP will win. The ones that aren't will lose.'

Intellectual property? Five years ago that phrase wasn't

> **KEY CONCEPT**
>
> Increasingly, companies that are good at managing IP will win. The one that aren't will lose.

even in the vocabulary of many CEOs, let alone a part of their business strategies. Indeed, many chief executives still regard patents, trademarks, copyrights, and other forms of intellectual property as legal matters best left to the corporate attorneys to fuss over while the CEOs concentrate on the truly strategic stuff of competitive warfare.

Not Thoman. Where others see mere legal instruments, he sees business tools. And where others see obscure pieces of paper gathering dust in the corporate legal office, he sees 'Rembrandts in the attic' waiting to be exploited for profit and competitive advantage.

To understand why Thoman thinks that way, you have to go back to his days as chief finance officer at IBM. There, he saw firsthand how an aggressive intellectual-property effort boosted annual patent-licensing royalties a phenomenal 3,300% – from £30 million in 1990 to nearly $1 billion to day. This $1 billion per year, it should be noted, is largely free cash cow – a recurring net revenue stream that represent one-ninth of IBM's annual pre-tax profits. The money goes straight to the bottom-line. To match that sort of net revenue stream, IBM would have to sell roughly $20 billion worth of additional products each year, or an amount equal to one-fourth its world-wide sales.

Source: Reprinted by permission of *Harvard Business Review* from 'Discovering new value in intellectual property' by Kevin G. Rivette and David Kline, January–February 2000, p. 56. Copyright © 2000 by the President and Fellows of Harvard College; all rights reserved.

Thoman's thinking is not new. Dow Chemical's efforts to catalogue nearly 30 000 patents brought it $40 million in savings and enabled the company to enter into $1 billion of new licensing agreements. Dow first began exploring new ways to manage intellectual assets five years ago.

The Internet, information technology and protection

According to the Millennium Message delivered by Dr Kamil Idris, Director General of WIPO:

A recent estimate suggests that the global Internet economy will rise to a value of US$3200 billion in 2003 – or less than half that if security and regulatory obstacles persist. Among such obstacles are the matters of domain names and trademarks on the Internet, which must be effectively protected if potential activity is to be maximised; the question of business process patenting whereby new methods of doing business over the Internet – such as 'reverse auctions' or 'one-click technology' are protected; the question of protection for digital items such as software, sound and video recordings which are relatively easily pirated on the Internet (the software industry alone cites current losses of US$11 billion per year); the question of database protection; and the question of maximising the potential of the medium for making patent information – the vast resource of all the world's millions of registered patents – easily available as reference materials to inventors around the world; all these are critical, and all are relevant to WIPO.

Encryption

Maintaining confidentiality has become and remains the biggest issue in the Internet age. A decade ago governments and large companies were the only users of encryption technology. Now, however, the technology is used by every kind of business and individuals wanting security on the Net.

Encryption is essential for developing confidence in the security of electronic transactions. Without such security, the growth of e-business will be dramatically curtailed. If, for example, a consumer books a holiday or buys furniture on the Internet and the web site has a mechanism for asking for payment by credit card, the consumer will be reluctant to give their card details without some assurance that the information will remain safe and confidential.

According to the Performance and Innovation Unit, encryption is very important for e-business. Encryption can be used to provide a variety of security services for commercial transactions. Principally these are integrity, authentication and confidentiality. *Integrity* services can guarantee that data has not been accidentally or deliberately corrupted; *authentication* guarantees that the originator or recipient of material is the person they claim to be; and *confidentiality* ensures that data cannot be read by anyone other than the intended recipients.

All these services are important to overcome the lack of trust felt by many people in the security of information sent over the Internet. This lack of trust is often cited as one of the most significant barriers to the increased use of electronic commerce.

Encryption can be used by business, for example, to guarantee:

- that contracts have not been improperly altered and have been signed by authorised personnel;
- that funds are transferred securely, by replacing information such as credit card details or account numbers in such a way that they cannot be used fraudulently;
- that market-sensitive information flowing between different parts of an organisation cannot be accessed by anyone other than those entitled to see it.

Encryption also has benefits in helping to protect the privacy of personal communications. Whether individuals are corresponding with friends using e-mail or electronically booking appointments with their doctor, some people will desire the added security that comes from encryption.

Case study: business use of encryption

The worldwide Automotive Network Exchange (ANX) is a system being developed collectively by vehicle manufacturers. It is a private network using Internet technologies (an extranet). The network binds together manufacturers, contractors, subcontractors and component suppliers throughout the industry supply chain. Through this network flow computer-aided design information and manufacturing files, purchase orders, shipment details, electronic payments and a wide variety of other business information. Encryption technology is used in a variety of ways:

• Integrity services assure that order information has not been corrupted.
• Authentication services assure that orders and invoices are genuine.
• Confidentiality services protect proprietary design information.

Encryption continues to make a significant contribution in areas such as the 72 per cent reduction in error rates experienced since the introduction of ANX.

Source: 'Encryption and law enforcement', A Performance and Innovation Unit Report, May 1999.

Whereas encryption is good for the growth of e-business, it has a downside to it in terms of its ability to conceal criminal and terrorist activities.

In 1999, Tony Blair, UK Prime Minister, set up a task force to look into the problems and nature of encryption. The task force made the following recommendations:

- The voluntary licensing of providers of encryption services will help improve consumer confidence and, therefore, support the development of e-commerce in the UK. However, these licensed providers should not be required to retain 'decryption keys' or to deposit them with third parties (i.e. no mandatory 'key escrow').
- The government should adopt a new approach based on co-operation with industry to balance the aim of giving the UK the world's best environment for e-commerce with the needs of law enforcement.
- A new government/industry joint forum should be established to discuss the development of encryption technologies and to ensure that the needs of law enforcement agencies are taken into account by the market.
- A new Technical Assistance Centre should be established, operating on a 24-hour basis to help law enforcement agencies derive intelligence from lawfully intercepted encrypted communications and lawfully retrieved stored data.
- The task force welcomes the intention to include in the forthcoming Electronic Commerce Bill provisions to allow lawful access to decryption keys and/or plain text under proper authority.
- The UK should encourage the development of an international framework, including a new forum, to deal with the impact of encryption on law enforcement.

The UK government is committed to developing electronic commerce. The pace of development around the world is unprecedented, but much depends on ensuring trust in this new medium and here encryption technologies have a vital role to play.[34]

The UK is one of the first countries in the world to legalise 'e-signatures', which English law now recognises as admissible in court. The Electronic Communications Act 2000 came into effect on 25 July and is intended to encourage the development of e-business in the UK. The new Act provides for a system of certification that is also admissible in court to support the authentication of e-signatures, but the problem of forgery remains.

Europe is also moving with the times to introduce various laws in keeping with the development of e-business. In September 2000 plans were approved in Strasbourg to allow e-commerce disputes to be resolved through Europe-wide small claims and alternative dispute resolution (ADR) procedures.

Biometric technology

On the Internet, goes the old gag, nobody knows you're a dog. The usual way to prove who you are when picking up e-mail, shopping online or visiting a closed area of a website is to type in a password – a surprisingly old-fashioned form of security that would be recog-

> **KEY CONCEPT**
>
> On the Internet, goes the old gag, nobody knows you're a dog. (*The Economist*)

nisable to a Roman soldier. But though passwords are simple, they are far from secure. Many people use the same one for everything. Worse, they may use a common word such as 'hello', their phone number or their dog's name – any of which could be guessed by an intruder.

Which is why some people champion a more high-tech approach. Rather than using a password to identify yourself to a computer, why not use a physical characteristic such as your voice, face or fingerprints? Such bodily measures, known as biometrics, have the appeal that they cannot be lost, forgotten or passed from one person to another and they are very hard to forge.[35]

Biometric technology could soon enter the market, which will boost the development of e-commerce.

A strategy for protection

E-business is about networks of partners. Many organisations hooking partners together in an extranet specify the types of routers, firewalls and security procedures that each partner has to have in order to safeguard the extranet connections.

Bruce Schneier makes the point that computer security is a matter of managing risk and like any other risk in business there should be a strategy for it.[36]

Key messages

- Some forms of knowledge have to be protected in order for organisations to sustain competitive advantage.
- Regulatory and legal frameworks facilitate knowledge transfer for the benefit of consumers.
- Intellectual property comes into existence when knowledge is embedded in products, processes and documents.
- It constitutes a group of strategic assets for the organisation.
- Intellectual property is protected by specialised organisations like the World Intellectual Property Organisation (WIPO).
- There are various conventions providing protection.
- In the absence of protection, organisations and individuals will be reluctant to share knowledge or to invest in research and development or innovation.

CONTINUED . . . **Key messages**

◆ The key categories of protection for intellectual property are patents, design registration, trade secrets, trademarks and copyright.

◆ The Internet has created special challenge for the authorities to stop organisations and individuals using information illegally.

◆ Information has to be secure if consumers are to deal over the Internet confidently and with trust.

◆ Security will promote the growth of e-business in the new economy.

◆ Encryption is a means of providing security. It should embody integrity, confidentiality and authentication.

◆ New technology, such as biometrics, is being explored to enhance security on the Internet.

Knowledge management in practice

The good news is that knowledge management is more than a fad some had predicted. The question now is, where is it headed? (Professor Thomas Davenport)

Overview

This chapter focuses on two organisations, Chevron Corporation and Sun Microsystems, in two distinct types of industry, and the way they use knowledge management to enhance their business performance.

The chapter highlights various lessons from the experiences of these companies.

Is knowledge management a fad? Some organisations feel that if they do not pay attention to knowledge management it will disappear and they will be able to continue to lead a 'normal' business life.

Some organisations are using knowledge to gain and sustain advantage. Knowledge

KEY CONCEPT

Knowledge is being used to improve products and processes and to leverage intellectual assets to gain competitive advantage.

is being used to improve products and processes and to leverage intellectual assets to gain competitive advantage. Knowledge management enables organisations to:

- become responsive to customer needs;
- stop reinventing the wheel;
- adopt best practices;
- innovate;
- retain talent;
- make decisions at speed;
- cut development time and time from 'lab to the market';
- gain new business.

Following are two cases of organisations that have used knowledge to improve key processes and enhance selling skills.

Case study: Chevron maps key processes and transfers best practices

by Verna Allee

Companies that share and seek out best practices demonstrate a visible dedication to the renewal of organizational knowledge. Chevron Corp., a leading proponent of this form of knowledge management, has already realized dramatic cost savings and important performance improvements through its 'best practices transfer' initiatives. Chevron chairman and CEO Ken Derr considers knowledge sharing of this sort 'the single most important' employee activity at the $36 billion company.

Chevron, which is based in San Francisco, has become a leading force in the emerging area of knowledge

CONTINUED ... Case study: Chevron maps key processes and transfers best practices

management by: strategically valuing knowledge; creatively using supporting technologies; specifically addressing and supporting knowledge creation, sharing and learning; and developing maps and frameworks that orient people to knowledge and information sources across the corporation.

Company executives expect such efforts to help it reach its stated aim of 10 per cent annual earnings growth – a target that won't be easy to hit considering that the world-wide market for oil and gas is expected to grow at an annual rate of just 2–3 per cent for the next 15–20 years.

Chevron is relying on strong growth in the developing world and production-related innovations such as horizontal drilling and three-dimensional, seismic exploration in order to meet its objectives. New markets and new technologies, however, will not be enough. If Chevron truly intends to meet its objectives, it must learn to effectively leverage and capitalise on knowledge on all fronts.

Fortunately, Derr is a vocal advocate of knowledge management (though the language used by him and others at Chevron usually revolves around the more conventional term, Best Practices Transfer). The company's commitment to learning and knowledge is central to 'The Chevron Way', a set of strategic statements that serve as a framework for company initiatives. One key element of the document is a commitment to learn 'faster and better than competitors through

KEY CONCEPT

Technology is also playing a key role in Chevron's knowledge management initiatives.

CONTINUED ... Case study: Chevron maps key processes and transfers best practices

benchmarking, sharing and implementing best practices, learning from experience, and continual individual learning and personal growth.'

Chevron relies on benchmarking and Total Quality Management (TQM) to engage in extensive internal knowledge sharing. The tools and processes of TQM have been a powerful vehicle for making tacit knowledge explicit. Process improvement techniques require in-depth, knowledge sharing in work groups and deliberate documentation of best practices and other critical corporate knowledge. Such problem-solving tools also provide a common language for creating and exchanging knowledge.

Technology is also playing a key role in Chevron's knowledge management initiatives. An important cornerstone for knowledge sharing is an innovative internal best practices database (which encourages people to contribute under the category 'good practice' – so as not to stifle important insights – as well as 'local best practice' – and 'industry best practice'). The company's Lotus Notes-based system allows people to pose questions to others throughout the company. They can also post learning and insights using key words and categories.

Furthermore, Chevron encourages interest in knowledge sharing by tracking and measuring the impact of best practices. The company examines the impact on corporate performance in terms of dollars saved, customer satisfaction, public favorability, and reduced cycle time. Harder to determine but also addressed are the degree of integration of best practices, the number of improved processes and usage on the database. Other

**CONTINUED . . . Case study: Chevron maps key
processes and transfers best practices**

knowledge sharing technologies include the intranet,
groupware such as Collabra Share, and e-mail.

And while many of the company's technical professionals will
continue to rely heavily on Lotus
Notes, the corporate intranet is
expected to become the most
important platform for communication and collaboration in the future.

> **KEY CONCEPT**
>
> The corporate intranet is expected to become the most important platform.

The intranet
incorporates such features as corporate and industry
news, human resources information, resources (such as
the best practices database and online training course),
financial information, and links to the home pages of
many Chevron businesses.

Although employees are certainly encouraged to make
use of networking technologies, yet another way of
encouraging knowledge sharing is through informal
networks that are the nucleus of 'communities of
practice'. These groups are provided minimal funding for
communication and occasional get-togethers. On a more
formal basis, the company sponsors regular internal
conferences for best practice exchange. Networks and
best practices groups may form either around technologies or around functional specialties. Some networks
address future trends or focus on emerging developments
in science and technology.

Chevron was one of the first companies to experiment
with knowledge mapping through the development of its
'Best Practice Resource Map' – a powerful tool that
serves as a kind of corporate 'yellow pages.' Roughly
following the focus areas of the Malcolm Baldrige

CONTINUED ... Case study: Chevron maps key processes and transfers best practices

assessment, the map identifies (through color coding) knowledge-based resources, teams and networks within the company. The map not only identifies key networks of people (under such categories as 'leadership', 'strategic planning', 'information and analysis', 'human resource development', 'process management', and 'customer focus and satisfaction') but also helps users find more traditional forms of knowledge such as library services. Roughly 5,000 copies of the original paper-based map were distributed.

More recently, under the continuing leadership of corporate quality consultant Gretna Lydecker, the resource map has been updated and adapted for the corporate intranet (dubbed 'go, chevron.com') with hot links to individual e-mail addresses for easy and instant contact. This approach encourages strong demand-pull since it is interactive and real-time. Cost effectiveness is high since linkages can be built quickly and easily for enriched connectivity. 'If you make it easy for people to network, they will.'

One key aspect of these efforts is their power to bring together a relatively dispersed and decentralised company. While the delegation of authority can lead to faster decision-making and greater customer-focus, it can also make it 'harder for people to share knowledge,' noted Derr in a speech on knowledge management. All companies, he added 'should be alert to conflicts between company structure and the imperative of sharing knowledge.'

Strong results

The implementation of best practice sharing initiatives has met with excellent results in multiple areas. For

CONTINUED . . . Case study: Chevron maps key processes and transfers best practices

instance, the company has adopted a best practice approach to managing its capital projects, which is a task accounting for $4 billion per year. After participating in benchmarking initiatives that enabled it to identify performance gaps, the company developed a new approach (known as 'Chevron Project Development and Execution Process') that has led to significant improvements. While Chevron admits that half its competitors used to manage capital projects more effectively than it did, it now claims to be one of the top performers. It claims to have saved $816 million in 'downstream' capital projects since 1992.

Greg Hanggi, consultant for Chevron Refining, points out that efforts to transfer best practices have helped this organisation overcome political and geographic barriers that once stood in the way of widespread productivity gains. It's an initiative that has been embraced by the refining area for about five years, producing both qualitative and quantitative benefits. Among other things, it has helped the refining teams develop new technologies and processes that cut the costs of sulfuric acid usage, which annually cost the company $50 million in years past, by $10 million.

There are several teams in the refining function that are now facilitated by a so-called 'master', a full-time participant hired by Chevron's Products business (which oversees the refining process) to ensure that tacit knowledge is made explicit and good ideas are shared. This individual is the driver and champion of best practice transfer – a knowledge manager that is considered 'the first point of contact' for people seeking knowledge and expertise.

CONTINUED . . . Case study: Chevron maps key processes and transfers best practices

Lessons learned? You can't 'push' best practices successfully. You have to support and nurture communities of specialists so that they form what Chevron calls 'self-discovering teams'.

> **KEY CONCEPT**
>
> You have to support and nurture communities of specialists so that they form what Chevron calls 'self-discovering teams'.

Whereas companies have traditionally focused on 'economies of scale', Hanggi points to the 'economies of knowledge' that have been achieved by bringing together technical specialists throughout the organisation. Such efforts, he says, have 'helped us move toward the development of a high performance organisation where people actively share information and knowledge.'

But there is more evidence of tangible payoff. Chevron USA Production reports savings of $30 million in 1996 on three best practice projects that focused on critical processes. Chevron also attributes much of its gains in energy-use management to knowledge sharing. The company has saved more than $650 million in energy efficiency since 1993 – thanks largely to the efforts of a network of people that evaluates company-wide energy costs. Moreover, best practice initiatives have indirectly helped the company realize $1.4 billion reduction in annual operating expenses in the last five years.

Finally, one must consider the way workgroups have begun to think strategically about knowledge. For example, the information management services group, which provides library and reference services for the company, developed a knowledge strategy to help it move from being a cost center to profit centre. It

CONTINUED . . . **Case study: Chevron maps key processes and transfers best practices**

is an initiative that I personally participated in as a consultant.

The unit faced a number of different challenges. Chevron employees were beginning to directly access corporate databases and other information providers. The information service group, which was being passed, faced competitive pressures for perhaps the first time. The group also was challenged to understand and support increasingly sophisticated and complex knowledge requests.

In response to these challenges, the group began to carve out a new direction – expanding its traditional library and information services to include value-added products and services that support knowledge building. As one team member put it, 'We have been acting as data order takers, but what our customers need are knowledge navigators. We need to focus on the added value we can bring by doing more.'

A key action step in this new direction was developing, publishing and distributing a service value 'portfolio' featuring services supporting knowledge creation at various levels. I worked with team leader Mary Ann Whitney and the rest of the group to create a guide for building knowledge products. Our efforts revolved around the customisation of knowledge. Understanding subtle differences in knowledge requests allowed the team to refine its services and provide higher value. It now offers packaged analysis, for instance, rather than mere information.

Four of the group's eight strategic goals grew directly out of this new way of thinking about its role in organizational knowledge creation and sharing. In

CONTINUED . . . Case study: Chevron maps key processes and transfers best practices

addition, the group began to identify its own knowledge and performance gaps. It found room for improvement in its documentation of core service work processes, contracting and consulting skills, and its level of expertise in complex analysis. As the group began to understand the different levels of knowledge work required for each product, it improved its cost estimates and gained more consistency in its deliverables.

As a result of the group's efforts, employee satisfaction with its services has measurably increased, it is expanding internal and external partnerships to add value, it is achieving recognition for its vital role in knowledge creation and it is developing new individual and team competencies for the future.

Chevron is an example of a company that provides what can be called a good 'practice field' for knowledge. The structures, technologies, and processes being implemented at Chevron allow a wide range of knowledge 'experiments' to take place. All of these efforts are supported by a culture of knowledge sharing. Through a continual process of experimentation and reflection, Chevron is generating the knowledge it needs for a competitive and profitable future.

As Derr sees it, knowledge management 'is something all companies have to master if they expect to compete in the global economy. Those who can learn quickly and then leverage and use that knowledge within the company will have a big advantage over those who can't.'

Source: Verna Allee @compuserve.com.http://webcom./ quantara/Chevron.html. Reprinted with permission.

In 1999, Chevron's net income was $2070 million, a 55 per cent increase over 1998; its sales was $36.6 billion, an 18 per cent increase over 1998.

Even before 2000 began, it was clear that a technology-driven 'new economy', led by the Internet, was profoundly changing the nature of business. Fearsomely volatile but rich in potential profits, this latest industrial revolution puts the Web at the centre of knowledge management and the efficient use of resources.

Not content to merely observe this historic trend, Chevron signaled it would aggressively participate in it. 'We're looking for places where our traditional oil and gas business and the new economy intersect,' says Don Paul, Chevron's vice-president of technology. 'At that nexus, we see opportunities for leadership in creating new value.'

To take advantage of these opportunities, the company formed Chevron Technology Ventures and Chevron eBusiness development Company (CeDC). Essentially mirror images of one another, one looks out and one looks in, mining that seam between old and new.' (Chevron Corporation 1999 Annual report)

Key lessons from the Chevron case study

- Chevron's strategy is to adopt and adapt best practices in order to achieve superior performance.
- It is using knowledge as a main driver of business performance.
- Leveraging knowledge has enabled the company to achieve significant savings in costs and improvement in business processes.
- It fosters a culture of knowledge creation and knowledge sharing and encourages learning.
- The commitment to focus on knowledge comes from the top.

■ Benchmarking is used to gather information on best practices and the focus of this practice is to enhance knowledge management throughout the organisation.

■ Traditional tools such as benchmarking, total quality management and continuous improvement are used to consolidate the practice of knowledge creation and knowledge sharing.

■ Technology is used as enabler.

■ Best-practice performance is measured and monitored.

■ The company deploys knowledge sharing technologies such as its intranet, groupware, Lotus Notes and e-mail.

■ The corporate intranet is used as a main platform of communication.

■ Informal get-togethers and the formation of communities of practice are actively encouraged.

■ Knowledge mapping is used to identify competencies, clusters of knowledge and resources.

■ The company constantly updates its knowledge maps with the help of a specifically appointed individual.

■ Employees have 'internalised' Chevron's knowledge management system.

■ The culture of Chevron encourages the formation of 'self-discovering teams' which enhances the creation of knowledge within the organisation.

■ Teams have been formed to embed knowledge into products and processes and to follow best practice.

■ The practice of knowledge management has resulted in staff satisfaction and employees' activities are adding value for Chevron's customers.

■ At Chevron knowledge management is a strategic issue.

■ Looking at the latest situation, Chevron is using its knowledge capability to compete in the new economy. It has entered the world of e-business.

Case study: Sun's knowledge network enhances its selling skills

by Britton Manasco

Scot McNealy, president and CEO of Sun Microsystems, has long believed that 'the network is the computer'. With the explosive growth of the Internet and the corporate intranet, those words have proved to be one of the most important technological prophesies of the era. Sun, to be sure, practices its faith. The $8 billion company, which has recently launched a powerful new knowledge system designed to strengthen it own sales processes, is demonstrating that networks are the future – and the future is now.

Sun, which is based in Mountain View, Calif., relies on its SunWEB intranet to link its 20,300 employees worldwide. At last count, the company had more than 1,000 internal Web servers putting up more than a quarter of a million Web and electronic pages. It claims to be saving $25 million a year on intranet distribution of documentation (which is only 5% of its total spending on documents). Furthermore, it is achieving big savings and enhancing its relationships with customers (and suppliers) by putting catalogs and technical information online.

Up until a year ago, however, the company had not given nearly enough thought to how it could use this powerful network to enhance the knowledge, skills, and capabilities of its employees and partners. That's when John Ryan, the field training manager for SunU (the company's employee development arm), and Kat Barclay, director of worldwide field training at Sun Microsystems Computer Co. (its computer sales division), began exploring opportunities for sales training and support on

> ### CONTINUED . . . Case study: Sun's knowledge network enhances its selling skills
>
> the Web. The vision is now becoming reality through the Internet-based knowledge and training system they now call 'SunTAN' – for training access network. Jerry Neece, a training programs manager for SunU, defines it as an 'interactive, network-based, curriculum management and sales support system'.
>
> The company's learning and knowledge needs are tremendous. A leading provider of hardware, software and services for enterprise intranets and Internet business ventures, Sun now generates 90% of its revenue from products that are less than one year old. It has consistently experienced widening product lines and shorter life cycles.
>
> As a result, the company found it could not train its sales professionals fast or effectively enough. It could no longer merely rely on traditional classroom-based training – a method that drags sales people away from their customers for days, overwhelms them with information and runs up high travel and lodging expenses. Sales training at HQ costs about $2,225 a week per individual (not counting lost sales time).
>
> Sun also realised it needed to make more training resources available to its people. While IBM and Hewlett-Packard were each giving new hires six weeks of training in their first six months of employment (and Digital Equipment was offering four), Sun was providing only one week. Sun sales personnel, as a result, were often less prepared than their competitors when they addressed customers. It was very important to help Sun sales people develop their knowledge and skills – without pulling them away from the field unnecessarily.

CONTINUED . . . Case study: Sun's knowledge network enhances its selling skills

That's where SunTAN comes in. The network, under the management of SunU, will consolidate sales training information, sales support resources, product updates and materials, competitive intelligence and an array of other content on the Sun intranet with an attractive and easy to use interface (complete with sand and umbrellas). One innovation that is making this all possible is Java, Sun's multimedia-oriented programming language that enables content authors to write a program once for viewing on any machine. While critics might argue that network bandwidth constraints ensure that such content is likely to be rather dull and static, Sun's pioneers in knowledge networking are seeking clever ways to deliver dynamic and engaging, Java-based content to the desktop – any time, and just about anywhere.

SunTAN's managers have developed a 'distributed learning architecture' based on a 'hierarchical storage management model'. In other words, they can ensure that the richest, most bandwidth-intensive and most actively used media – say, a video demonstrating Sun's new line of server products – is distributed to and stored on a local server at a regional sales office rather than at the company's headquarters. Rather than centralizing all resources in one place and then inviting sales people to access it with everything from T1 lines to 28.8 kbps modems, SunTAN operators can upload them and users can download them (usually during non-peak hours) to local servers – allowing for faster connections and richer media such as video, audio and animation.

As the content becomes more compelling, the benefits of classroom training will be steadily outweighed by the

CONTINUED . . . Case study: Sun's knowledge network enhances its selling skills

benefits of learning on-demand. While lectures can certainly be stored as video, the new media will enable users to escape the monotonous, sequential presentation of information. It might even be, well, engaging. In fact desktop training programs may soon look like enhanced television: MPEG-2 video, 30 frames per second, digital sound. 'We can start to do some things in training that people are apologising for not being able to do now,' says Neece.

Indeed SunTan promises to transform the company's learning processes. 'In the new way of distance learning, you no longer have to retain knowledge,' he adds. 'The only knowledge that you have to retain is knowledge of the location of where you can go to get information when you need it. It changes so often that there is no need to retain it – except for the key information that determines how you make 80% of your sales. It's a pull rather than a push model.'

Most importantly, SunTAN promises to enhance the effectiveness and productivity of sales personnel. 'I think the sales force knows the server product line pretty well and they know the desktop line because 80% of our revenue comes from those products,' says Neece. 'But what about the other products? When you need to know, you want to find information on them quickly. I think it will help generate a lot of revenue. Take the 80/20 rule. If 20% of your products do 80% of the revenue, you can increase the revenue of that 80% of the products through something like SunTAN.'

The network, however, is just now being rolled out and is not yet widely used in Sun. 'I think it will have a significant impact on the use of the intranet to get current information that one needs for sales and the options that one needs to increase one's sales abilities,' says Barclay, SMCC's field training director. 'But we have some distance to go. We are changing a method of accessing training and knowledge – something that just hasn't been done this way before. It is not an easy transition. There is a lot of interest in it and a lot of excitement about it, but there is going to have to be a great deal of promotional activity within Sun.'

Funding and payback

Where is the money for SunTAN's development coming from? Neece says that he is reinvesting much of the revenue from his SunU new hire training – about $240,000 per quarter (earned through charges to other Sun divisions, especially SMCC) – in the project. The project also is being funded directly by MSCC's worldwide field training group.

Where's the payback? The payback lies in SunTAN's potential to dramatically enhance the effectiveness of sales people while cutting the costs associated with training them in the conventional fashion. The system will soon begin paying for itself when it reduces the number of trips back to HQ for training. By reducing the number of annual sales training trips by one (from, say, six to five) for its sales engineers, Sun realizes hard, tangible savings of $3.5 million annually. And, considering that sales personnel now number more than 3,500 at Sun, the annual savings for the entire sales force could rise to 47.5 million.

CONTINUED ... Case study: Sun's knowledge network enhances its selling skills

The more intangible gains are also significant. SunTAN acts as a just-in-time knowledge or performance support system – enabling sales personnel to rapidly access critical information while they have a customer on the phone. Moreover, Sun sales people need not abandon their customers for a week in order to train. They can engage in sales training in a sales-directed way at their desktops (or at home) – and, if a customer calls with a problem or request, they are still accessible. As Neece put it, 'What's it worth to have sales rep or sales engineer still back there in the branch when the customer has that big problem? There is a soft dollar value there that is difficult to measure but is nevertheless there.'

While SunTAN was originally developed for Sun's direct sales reps and sales engineers, it is now available to the company's 20,000 resellers who account for more than 60% of worldwide sales. Soon, it will also be available to independent software vendors and commercial systems integrators such as EDS, Andersen, Perot Systems, Oracle and SAP.

What emerges from the SunTAN effort and similar ones now underway in the corporate world can be expected to significantly enhance the productivity of knowledge workers in the years to come. And, considering

KEY CONCEPT

Of course, it often hurts to be on the bleeding edge. 'I think we are taking many of the arrows and doing most of the bleeding for a lot of other people,' says Neece.

that Sun is selling the products and services that are enabling companies to develop knowledge networks, it is likely to play an influential role in their adoption.

Source: *Knowledge Inc.*, May 1997. Reprinted with permission.

Key lessons from the Sun case study

- Knowledge management does not have to be applied to all the functional divisions of the organisation.
- The network facilitates communication with employees and enables information sharing.
- The Internet is playing a key role in distributing information.
- Networks can be leveraged to create knowledge.
- Intranet-based training is creating much needed training for sales staff. Such training has a dramatic effect on reducing training costs.
- Sun's knowledge management system reflects how information can be transformed into knowledge to enhance the competencies of its staff.
- A knowledge management system can be used to bring a learning culture into the organisation.
- Knowledge management has a favourable impact on bottom-line results.
- The gains of knowledge management are tangible as well as intangible.
- Before becoming a leading-edge organisation in terms of knowledge management, it may be inevitable initially to operate on the 'bleeding edge'.

Becoming a knowledge-driven organisation

CHAPTER 12

The entrepreneur is essentially a visualizer and an actualizer.
He can visualize something, and when he visualizes it he
sees exactly how to make it happen. (Robert L. Schwartz)

Overview

This chapter provides a checklist of what to do in order
to become a knowledge-driven organisation. It is a
synthesis of all the other chapters.

There is also a questionnaire to enable you to assess
to what extent you are a knowledge-driven organisation.

Making knowledge the DNA of your organisation

Organisations must appreciate the importance of information.
Information on customers, suppliers, staff and other partners
as well as information on competitors and the way they do
business constitute a business's intangible assets.

IMPLEMENTATION CHECKLIST

◆ Use the Internet to gain and exchange information. Capture all key information via the Internet.

◆ Build an extranet to create networks and to share information.

◆ Appreciate the importance of your employees. There is a significant proportion of tacit and explicit knowledge embodied in your employees that should be used to gain superior performance.

◆ Staff should be encouraged to share their knowledge by documenting their experiences, by conversations, by brainstorming and so on.

◆ There should be technology in place to enable the sharing and transfer of knowledge. Many organisations have intranets with firewalls to provide security for their information.

◆ Create a directory of employees' competencies and their unique experiences and skills. Make this information accessible so that expertise can be identified very quickly.

◆ To motivate staff to share their knowledge, encourage a culture of empowerment. Knowledge is power. Let employees empower one another by sharing their knowledge.

◆ Create initiatives that act as a focal point for the creation and use of knowledge. In the case of Microsoft, the focal point was identifying key competencies.

◆ Consider the benefits that your organisation can gain by using knowledge and incorporate these benefits in your business plan.

◆ Appoint someone or a small group of individuals to champion the cause of knowledge management.

◆ Start by deciding to become a learning organisation. To do so requires mastery of five disciplines: personal mastery, mental models, shared vision, team learning and systems thinking.

Personal mastery

◆ Encourage your staff to constantly review their skills.
◆ Provide opportunities for training and development.
◆ Encourage individuals to examine and develop themselves. Training in the area of developing assertiveness, interpersonal skills and neurolinguistic programming helps promote self awareness.
◆ Self-development generates inner energy to help individuals achieve their personal goals within the context of the organisation.
◆ Personal mastery fosters trust and enhances individual capability, both of which are key drivers of knowledge creation and knowledge sharing.

Mental models

◆ Mental models are individual perceptions of the world and the organisation. Such perceptions affect individual behaviour. In a changing world, individuals constantly have to examine their mental models and adapt them to meet the needs of the environment.
◆ Sharing of information and experiences helps shape our mental models.
◆ In the age of the Internet, there is a danger that face-to-face and interpersonal communication could suffer. It is important, whenever possible, to provide the opportunity for individuals to meet face to face so that they can relate to one another when they communicate via e-mail or an extranet.

♦ Organisations should provide an environment for individuals to meet and share their experiences and exchange information.

Shared vision

♦ For superior performance and for the organisation to recruit and retain appropriate talent, individual and organisational values and visions have to be congruent. Articulate and communicate widely your organisation's values and vision and ascertain at the time of recruitment an individual's values and vision.

Team learning

♦ Teams create synergy. Learning in a team creates relationships, trust and shared vision. Teams, like organisations, have to have objectives and a sense of purpose.

♦ Team learning takes place when members trust one another and feel comfortable with the values and vision of the organisation. Team learning, be it real or virtual, is important to generate and share knowledge.

♦ Electronically connected knowledge workers need to learn how to work together and how to harness their collective knowledge.

Systems thinking

♦ A leader needs systems thinking to integrate all key disciplines of the learning organisation. The organisation's core competence is determined by the existence of systems thinking. This is what effective leadership is all about.

Once the organisation gets into the learning organisation mode it can start using knowledge to gain competitive advantage. Use of knowledge will release energy within the organisation and this energy will drive the business forward to achieve superior performance.

To use knowledge organisations have to create situations to transform information into knowledge. Such situations include 'learning by doing', prototyping, creation and management of brands, embedding knowledge into products and processes and benchmarking for best practice.

Such situations can be facilitated by the use of technology, especially the Internet.

 ## IMPLEMENTATION CHECKLIST:
knowledge and e-business

- E-business is a phenomenon of the new economy.
- It operates in an environment that is complex and fast changing.
- Because of this complexity it requires new ways of thinking and doing business in a competitive arena where rules are changing constantly.
- Complexity and uncertainty favour the development of networks and alliances.
- Working in a network environment (linking producers, distributors and customers) create synergy, which constitutes an intangible asset of the business. This intangible asset underpins successful business performance.
- The use of knowledge is imperative for an e-business to come up with an innovative value chain that can deliver speed, cut the cost of operations and create effective relationships with customers.
- Such a value chain has to deliver benefits in four areas, namely *finance* (cutting costs, enhance revenues), *processes* (promoting concurrent business transactions and business link-ups, for example), *people* (recruiting and retaining talent) and *customers* (satisfaction and loyalty).

◆ Measurement has to be focused on all these four areas in order to assess whether the organisation is achieving its strategic objectives.

◆ E-business strategy should not focus on funding alone but must incorporate the four Ps: – people (employees and customers), products, processes and profit.

◆ The business plan emerging from the strategy should address these four strategic strands of business.

◆ Knowledge management enables an e-business to use information and to measure and increase the value of customers.

◆ Businesses that are using interactive intranets are leapfrogging their competitors.

Conclusion

The 7 S framework is very useful for focusing attention on where knowledge can be leveraged and to remind us how all seven key areas are significantly inter-related.

 IMPLEMENTATION CHECKLIST

◆ *Strategy* – the e-business's strategy has to be underpinned by innovative strategic thinking.

◆ *Systems* – systems have to be put in place to achieve strategic goals.

◆ *Structure* – structure and systems have to accommodate network relationships.

◆ *Shared value* – the organisation's values and vision have to be communicated and its culture has to promote innovation and empower people to make key decisions for their development and for business success.

- *Staff* – given the existence of a 'war for talent', top management has to be involved in recruitment. Appropriate talent is crucial to business success.
- *Skills* – skills have to be monitored and enhanced constantly.
- *Style* – the leadership style has to be that of a servant-leader. That is, a leader should serve their people in acting as a coach and a mentor.

 PAUSE FOR THOUGHT

Organisations are perfectly designed for the results they achieve. (Paul Gustavson)

Assessing your organisation's culture for knowledge management

Scoring

This questionnaire is divided into three sections, organisational, operational and personal.

Score each question on a scale of 1 to 5, as follows:

I strongly agree	I tend to agree	I am not sure	I tend to disagree	I strongly disagree
1	2	3	4	5

Corporate perspective

1 Our organisation has a mission statement.

1	2	3	4	5

2 Everyone or most employees know our organisation's mission statement.

1	2	3	4	5

3   Our strategy/strategic objectives are communicated to all
    employees.

    I   2   3   4   5

4   Knowledge sharing is one of our key strategic objectives.

    I   2   3   4   5

5   The type of knowledge required to achieve out strategic
    goals is communicated throughout the organisation.

    I   2   3   4   5

6   Our strategic planning involves all departments/division/
    team heads.

    I   2   3   4   5

7   Our organisation's mission statement is very clearly
    expressed.

    I   2   3   4   5

8   The importance of knowledge is communicated to
    everyone in our organisation.

    I   2   3   4   5

9   Our organisation invests in a knowledge management
    system.

    I   2   3   4   5

10 All departments/sections in our organisation have clear
    and specific objectives.

    I   2   3   4   5

11 Our chief executive/managing director has credibility
    within our organisation.

    I   2   3   4   5

12 Our organisation captures all key information on our
    customers.

    I   2   3   4   5

13 We use an intranet or other method to get and transfer information.

    1   2   3   4   5

14 We have free access to information on our organisation by approaching appropriate individuals/departments.

    1   2   3   4   5

15 We have access to information on our customers and alliance partners.

    1   2   3   4   5

16 We have access to information on the experiences and competencies of our key staff.

    1   2   3   4   5

17 Our organisation undertakes analysis of its external environment.

    1   2   3   4   5

18 All departments/divisions/teams are expected to make a contribution to the external environmental analysis.

    1   2   3   4   5

19 All information is updated regularly.

    1   2   3   4   5

20 All jobs in our organisation are clearly defined.

    1   2   3   4   5

21 There is good communication in our organisation between departments/sections/teams.

    1   2   3   4   5

22 Our chief executive officer/managing director is a 'visible' figure in our organisation.

    1   2   3   4   5

23 We trust our chief executive officer/managing director.

    1   2   3   4   5

24 We are kept informed of our organisation's performance on a regular basis.

 1   2   3   4   5

25 All/most employees are highly committed to the strategic goals of our organisation.

 1   2   3   4   5

26 We/most of us are very proud to work for our organisation.

 1   2   3   4   5

27 Our organisation values its people.

 1   2   3   4   5

28 Our organisation recognises people for doing good work.

 1   2   3   4   5

29 We are encouraged to express our views on management and performance in relation to our organisation.

 1   2   3   4   5

30 Our strategy incorporates meeting customer satisfaction.

 1   2   3   4   5

31 Our chief executive/managing director visits some of our customers.

 1   2   3   4   5

32 Our organisation tries to align customer satisfaction with employee satisfaction.

 1   2   3   4   5

33 Our company believes in staff training.

 1   2   3   4   5

34 Our company spends a proportion of its revenue on staff training.

 1   2   3   4   5

35 Before undertaking staff training our organisation does a training needs analysis.

    1   2   3   4   5

36 In assessing training needs all employees are consulted.

    1   2   3   4   5

37 Our organisation keeps in close contact with some of our key customers.

    1   2   3   4   5

38 Our organisation keeps in close contact with our suppliers.

    1   2   3   4   5

39 Our organisation considers our suppliers as partners.

    1   2   3   4   5

40 Our organisation constantly reviews the process of delivering customer service.

    1   2   3   4   5

41 Our organisation constantly reviews the process of product/service delivery.

    1   2   3   4   5

42 Our organisation encourages creativity among staff.

    1   2   3   4   5

43 Inside our organisation we treat each other as customers.

    1   2   3   4   5

44 If we hear any bad comments about our organisation we tell our boss.

    1   2   3   4   5

45 Our organisation considers the interests of direct stakeholders.

    1   2   3   4   5

46 Our organisation listens to its customers.

   1   2   3   4   5

Operational perspective

1 My manager/supervisor/team leader sets performance goals for us.

   1   2   3   4   5

2 Sharing knowledge is one of our performance goals.

   1   2   3   4   5

3 We work as a team in our department.

   1   2   3   4   5

4 We communicate with one another in our department.

   1   2   3   4   5

5 We get good support from our manager/supervisor/team leader.

   1   2   3   4   5

6 Mistakes are tolerated in our department.

   1   2   3   4   5

7 Our manager/supervisor/team leader is very approachable.

   1   2   3   4   5

8 Our manager/supervisor/team leader keeps us informed of the progress of our department.

   1   2   3   4   5

9 We can always rely on getting help and advice from our manager/supervisor/team leader.

   1   2   3   4   5

10 In our department we help each other, when necessary.

   1   2   3   4   5

11 We record our experiences for the benefit of other colleagues.

    1   2   3   4   5

12 We have clear information on what we are expected to do.

    1   2   3   4   5

13 We have clear performance goals in our department.

    1   2   3   4   5

14 We are involved in setting our own performance goals.

    1   2   3   4   5

15 Our individual/team performance goals are linked with the overall organisation's goals.

    1   2   3   4   5

16 Our goals are monitored every three/six months.

    1   2   3   4   5

17 We have performance appraisals every three/six months.

    1   2   3   4   5

18 We are given time to prepare for our appraisals.

    1   2   3   4   5

19 We know exactly what our standards of performance should be.

    1   2   3   4   5

20 We look forward to our performance appraisals.

    1   2   3   4   5

21 We are given information on our strengths and weaknesses at our appraisals.

    1   2   3   4   5

22 Our appraisals are used to develop our training programmes.

    1   2   3   4   5

23   We get very quick feedback from our appraisals.

    1   2   3   4   5

24   Our manager/supervisor/team leader is very good at giving positive and constructive feedback after appraisals.

    1   2   3   4   5

25   The feedback from our appraisals incorporates an action plan.

    1   2   3   4   5

26   Our manger/supervisor/team leader gives us recognition for good performance.

    1   2   3   4   5

27   We are encouraged to establish relationships with our business partners.

    1   2   3   4   5

28   Our manager/supervisor/team leader is available to help us, when necessary.

    1   2   3   4   5

29   We have clearly defined responsibilities in our department.

    1   2   3   4   5

30   We have regular meetings in our department.

    1   2   3   4   5

31   We trust our manager/supervisor/team leader.

    1   2   3   4   5

Personal perspective

1   I plan my own personal development.

    1   2   3   4   5

2   I am proud of my organisation.

    1   2   3   4   5

3 I trust my colleagues.

1   2   3   4   5

4 I share all my experiences.

1   2   3   4   5

5 I can manage my time properly.

1   2   3   4   5

6 I do not work long hours.

1   2   3   4   5

7 I do not find my work very stressful.

1   2   3   4   5

8 I do not take work home regularly.

1   2   3   4   5

9 If I am stressed I can discuss my situation with my colleagues.

1   2   3   4   5

10 I can approach my manager/supervisor/team leader if I have any problems.

1   2   3   4   5

11 I can approach my manager/supervisor/team leader if I have good ideas for the department.

1   2   3   4   5

12 I like working for my department.

1   2   3   4   5

13 I can get training in acquiring new skills if I ask for it.

1   2   3   4   5

14 My values are congruent with the values of the organisation.

1   2   3   4   5

Organisational perspective scoring

46 points. Excellent. Your Organisation has an appropriate culture and is managed very well. It is well placed to undertake a balanced performance approach and consider the needs of all stakeholders.

47–56 points. Very good. Your organisation is managed well but it could do better. It is well placed to undertake meaningful performance management.

57–65 points. Good. Your organisation is well placed to improve significantly and manage its performance effectively.

66–77 points. Average. If it is not careful, your organisation will end up badly managed and lose its competitive strength.

78–97 points. Bad. Your organisation has an opportunity to improve significantly by paying attention to its strategy formulation and the interests of all its direct stakeholders.

98–182 points. Very bad. Your organisation is very badly managed. It has short-term survival prospects.

183+ points. Extremely bad. Your organisation has a total disregard for its people and other stakeholders. I am surprised it still exists.

 PAUSE FOR THOUGHT

Many organisations work efficiently but not effectively. To be effective organisations have to work efficiently to achieve their corporate objectives. These objectives should embrace the interests of shareholders and other stakeholders, including customers, employees and partners.

To become effective in a fast-changing business world organisations have to manage knowledge.

To become a knowledge-driven organisation you have to audit key dimensions of business such as use of knowledge, leadership, competencies, processes and relationships.

Operational perspective scoring

31–35 points. Excellent. Your department is excellent. However, to be effective this score has to match a very low score on the organisational perspective.

36–61 points. Very good. Your department has very good potential of achieving excellent status. Again, consistency with a low score on the organisational perspective is important.

62–92 points. Good. Your department scores an average performance. It has the potential to improve significantly.

93–122 points. Bad. Your department is managed badly. If it is achieving its desired results now these results will not be sustained.

122+ points. Very bad. The morale and the staff turnover of your department must be very poor.

 PAUSE FOR THOUGHT

To be effective and sustain good results, departmental objectives and results must be consistent with organisational objectives.

Personal perspective scoring

14–16 points. You have excellent self-management skill.

17–20 points. You manage yourself very well.

21–30 points. You manage yourself fairly well.

31–40 points. You must improve your self-management style to perform effectively.

41+ points. You have a very bad self-management style.

 PAUSE FOR THOUGHT

Personal effectiveness has to be results oriented in order to improve organisational capability.

Your action plan

Ten things I am going to do to help us become a knowledge-driven organisation

1 _____

2 _____

3 _____

4 _____

5 _____

6 _____

7 _____

8 _____

9 _____

10 _____

NOTES

1   'The new economy survey', *The Economist*, 23 September 2000, p. 33.
2   The Economist Conferences Scenario Planning Seminar, 19 February
     1993.
3   Colin Barrow, Robert Brown and Liz Clarke (1992) *The Business
     Growth Handbook*, London: Kogan Page, p. 100.
4   *Harvard Business Review*, Mar.–Apr. 1998, p. 59.
5   Ibid., p. 69.
6   *Business Week*, 4 September 2000.
7   'Fast Track', *Sunday Times*, 3 December 2000.
8   Ron Zemke and Tom Connellan (2000) *E-Service: 24 Ways to Keep Your
     Customers When Competition Is Just a Click Away*, New York: Amacom.
9   *Harvard Business Review*, Jan.–Feb. 1992.
10   Peter Drucker (1964) Managing for Results, London: Butterworth
     Heinemann, p. 104.
11   Georg von Krogh, Johan Roos and Dirk Kleine (eds) *Knowing in
     Firms*, London: Sage, Chapter 6.
12   The Economist Conferences Seminar, 1995.
13   Robert Bruce Shaw (1997) *Trust in the Balance*, San Francisco, CA:
     Jossey-Bass, p. 18.
14   Peter Drucker (1989) *The New Realities*, London: Butterworth
     Heinemann.
15   Ettienne C. Wenger and William M. Snyder (2000) 'Communities of
     practice: the organizational frontier', *Harvard Business Review*, May–
     June, p. 139.
16   Ned Hermann (1996) *The Whole Brain Business Book*, New York:
     McGraw-Hill.
17   Peter Cappelli (2000) 'A market-driven approach to retaining talent',
     Harvard Business Review, Jan.–Feb., p. 104.
18   Jerald Greenberg and Robert A. Baron (2000) *Behavior in Organizations*,
     Englewood Cliffs, NJ: Prentice Hall.
18   *CIO Web Business*, 1 May 1999.
19   *Sunday Times*, 20 July 2000.
20   *Digital Britain* (2000) Microsoft Corporation.
21   Ibid.
22   Kevin Jones, *Inter@ctive Week*, 24 February 1998.

23 Frederick Reichheld and Phil Schefter (2000) 'E-loyalty: your secret weapon on the Web', *Harvard Business Review*, Jul.–Aug., p. 106.
24 Peter Drucker (1985) *Innovation and Entrepreneurship*, London: Butterworth Heinemann, p. 17.
25 Andrew Hargadon and Robert I. Sutton (2000) 'Building an innovation factory', *Harvard Business Review*, May–Jun.
26 Ibid.
27 Rosabeth Moss Kanter (1984) *The Change Masters: Innovation and Entrepreneurship in the American Corporation*, New York: Simon and Schuster.
28 Gary Hamel (2000) 'Re-invent your company', *Fortune*, 12 June, p. 105.
29 Michael Skapinker (2000) 'Think small for success', *Digital Britain*, Microsoft Corporation.
30 Morten T. Hansen, Nitin Nohria and Thomas Tierney (1999) 'What's your strategy for managing knowledge?', *Harvard Business Review*, Mar.–Apr.
31 D. Kolb (1984) *Experiential Learning: Experience as the Source of Learning and Development*, Englewood Cliffs, NJ: Prentice Hall.
32 Peter M. Senge (1993) *The Fifth Discipline: The Art and Practice of the Learning Organization*, New York: Random House.
33 Peter Drucker (1995) *Managing in a Time of Great Change*, London: Butterworth Heinemann.
34 'Encryption and law enforcement', A Performance and Innovation Unit Report, May 1999.
35 *The Economist*, 9 September 2000.
36 Bruce Schneier (2000) *Secrets and Lies: Digital Security in a Networked World*, Chichester: Wiley.

BIBLIOGRAPHY

Abell, Angela and Oxbrow, Nigel (1999) 'Skills for the knowledge economy: the reality of the marketplace', *Business Information Review*, 16(3, Sept.): 115–21.

Albert, Steven and Bradley, Keith (1997) *Managing Knowledge: Experts, Agencies and Organizations*, Cambridge: Cambridge University Press.

Allday, Deborah (1998) *Spinning Straw into Gold: Managing Intellectual Capital Effectively*, London: Institute of Management.

Apostolou, Dimitris and Mentzas, Gregory (1999) 'Managing corporate knowledge: a comparative analysis of experiences in consulting firms, Part 1', *Knowledge and Process Management*, 6(3): 129–38.

Armistead, Colin (1999) 'Knowledge management and process performance', *Journal of Knowledge Management*, 3(2): 143–54.

Baladi, Peter (1999) 'Knowledge and competence management: Ericsson Business Consulting', *Business Strategy Review*, 10(4, Winter): 20–28.

Barker, Mike (2000) 'Knowledge management best practice', *Personnel Today*, 29 Feb.: 17.

Bater, Bob (1999) 'Knowledge management: a model approach', *Managing Information*, 6(8, Oct.): 38–41.

Bennett, Roger and Gabriel, Helen (1999) 'Organisational factors and knowledge management within large marketing departments: an empirical study', *Journal of Knowledge Management*, 3(3): 212–25.

Birchall, David W. and Tovstiga, George (1999) 'The strategic potential of a firm's knowledge portfolio', *Journal of General Management*, 25(1, Autumn): 1–16.

Bokin, Jim (1999) *Smart Business: How Knowledge Communities Can Revolutionize your Company*, New York, NY: Free Press.

Bonfield, Sir Peter (1999) 'Knowledge management strategy at BT', *Managing Information*, 6(6, Jul/Aug.): 26–30.

Bonner, Dede (2000) 'Enter the chief knowledge officer', *Training and Development USA*, 54(2): 36–40.

Bowander, B. and Miyake, T. (2000) 'Technology strategy of Toshiba Corporation: a knowledge evolution perspective', *International Journal of Technology Management*, 19(7/8): 864–95.

Bresman, Henrik, Birkinshaw, Julian and Nobel, Robert (1999) 'Knowledge transfer in international acquisitions', *Journal of International Business Studies*, 30(3): 439–62.

Buckley, Peter J. and Carter, Martin J. (2000) 'Knowledge management in global technology markets: applying theory to practice', *Long Range Planning*, 33(1, Feb): 55–71.

Bukowitz, Wendi and Williams, Ruth L. (1999) *The Knowledge Management Fieldbook*, Harlow: Pearson Education.

Burton Jones, Alan (1999) *Knowledge Capitalism: Business Work and Learning in the New Economy*, Oxford: Oxford University Press.

Carneiro, Alberto (2000) 'How does knowledge management influence innovation and competitiveness?', *Journal of Knowledge Management*, 4(2): 87–98.

Centre for Strategic Business Studies (1998) *Managing Knowledge and Intellectual Capital*, Winchester: CSBS Publications.

Chait, Laurence P. (1999) 'Creating a successful knowledge management system', *Journal of Business Strategy*, 20(2, Mar./Apr.): 23–6.

Chase, Rory L. (1998) *Creating a Knowledge Management Business Strategy: Delivering Bottom Line Results*, Lavendon: Management Trends International.

Chase, Rory, L. (1999) *Most Admired Knowledge Enterprises Report*, Lavendon: Management Trends International.

Coles, Margaret (1999) 'Knowing is succeeding', *Director*, 52(8, Mar.): 60–63.

Cotter, Nick, Bagshaw, Mike and Bagshaw, Caroline (1999) 'Intellectual capital: knowledge has a value', *Training Journal*, Apr.: 10–12.

Coulson-Thomas, Colin (1998) 'Knowledge is power', *Chartered Secretary*, Jan.: 24–5.

Cropley, Jacqueline (1998) 'Knowledge management: a dilemma', *Business Information Review*, 15(1, Mar.): 27–34.

Davenport, Thomas H., De Long, David W. and Beers, Michael C. (1998) 'Successful knowledge management projects', *Sloan Management Review*, 39(2, Winter): 43–57.

de Jager, Martha (1999) 'The KMAT benchmarking knowledge management', *Library Management*, 20(7): 367–72.

Dixon, Nancy (2000) 'The insight track', *People Management*, 6(4, 17 Feb.): 34–9.

Dixon, Nancy M. (1999) 'Changing face of knowledge', *Learning Organization Journal*, 6(5): 212–16.

Dixon, Nancy M. (2000) *Common Knowledge: How Companies Thrive by Sharing What They Know*, Boston, MA: Harvard Business School Press.

Dove, Rick (1999) 'Knowledge management: response ability and the agile enterprise', *Journal of Knowledge Management*, 3(1): 18–35.

Fisher, Kimball and Fisher, Mareen Duncan (1998) *The Distributed Mind:*

Achieving High Performance Through the Collective Intelligence of Knowledge Work Teams, New York, NY: Amacom.

Foster, Faren (1999) 'Justifying knowledge management investments', *Knowledge and Process Management*, 6(3): 154–7.

Fruin, W. Mark (1997) *Knowledge Works: Managing Intellectual Capital at Toshiba*, Oxford: Oxford University Press.

Gladstone, Bryan (2000) *From Know How to Knowledge: the Essential Guide to Understanding and Implementing Knowledge Management*, London: Industrial Society.

Greco, Joann (1999) 'Knowledge is power', *Journal of Business Strategy*, 20(2, Mar./Apr.): 18–22.

Gross, Neil (2000) 'Mining a company's mother lode of talent', *International Business Week*, 21 Aug.: 70–71.

Gupta, Anil K. and Gouindarajan (2000) 'Knowledge management's social dimension: lessons from Nucor Steel', *Sloan Management Review*, 42(1, Fall): 71–80.

Hansen, Morten T., Nohria, Nitin and Tiernay, Thomas (1999) 'What's your strategy for managing knowledge?', *Harvard Business Review*, 77(2, Mar./Apr.): 106–16.

Havens, Charnell and Knap, Ellen (1999) 'Easing into knowledge management', *Strategy and Leadership*, 27(2, Mar./Apr.): 4–9.

Hildreth, Paul, Kimble, Chris and Wright, Peter (2000) 'Communities of practice in the distributed international environment', *Journal of Knowledge Management*, 4(1): 27–37.

Hull, Richard, Coombs, Rod and Peltu, Malcolm (2000) 'Knowledge management practices for innovation: an audit tool for improvement', *International Journal of Technology Management*, 20(5–8): 633–56.

Huseman, Richard C. and Goodman, Jon P. (1999) *Leading with Knowledge: the Nature of Competition in the 21st Century*, Thousand Oaks, CA: Sage.

Kermally, Sultan (1990) *When Economies Means Business*, London: FT Management.

Kermally, Sultan (1996) *Total Management Thinking*, Oxford: Butterworth-Heinemann.

Klein, David A. (1998) *The Strategic Management of Intellectual Capital*, Boston, MA: Harvard Business School Press.

Knight, Daniel J. (1999) 'Performance measures for increasing intellectual capital', *Strategy and Leadership*, 27(2, Mar./Apr.): 22–7.

Koulopoulos, Thomas M. and Frappaolo, Carl (1999) *Smart Things to Know about Knowledge Management*, Oxford: Capstone.

KPMG Management Consulting (1998) *Knowledge Management: Research Report*, London: KPMG.

KPMG Management Consulting (1998) *The Power of Knowledge: a Business Guide to Knowledge Management*, London: KPMG.

Lahti, Ryan K. and Beyerlein, Michael M. (2000) 'Knowledge transfer and

management consulting: a look at the firm', *Business Horizons*, 43(1, Jan./
Feb.): 65–74.

Liebowitz, Jay et al. (2000) 'Knowledge audit', *Knowledge and Process
Management*, 7(1): 3–10.

Lucas, Erika (2000) 'Creating a give and take culture', *Professional Manager*,
9(3, May): 11–13.

Macdonald, John (1999) *Understanding Knowledge Management in a Week*,
London: Hodder and Stoughton.

Martensson, Maria (2000) 'Critical review of knowledge management as a
management tool', *Journal of Knowledge Management*, 4(3): 204–16.

Mayo, Andrew (1999) 'The trainer and knowledge management', *Training
Journal*, Apr.: 6–9.

McAdam, Rodney (2000) 'Knowledge management as a catalyst for
innovation within organizations: a qualitative study', *Knowledge and
Process Management*, 7(4): 233–41.

McAdam, Rodney and McCreedy, Sandra (1999) 'A critical review of
knowledge management models', *Learning Organization Journal*, 6(3): 91–
100.

McAdam, Rodney and McCreedy, Sandra (2000) 'A critique of knowledge
management using a social constructionist model', *New Technology and
Employment*, 15(2, Sept.): 155–68.

McCampbell, Atefeh Sadri, Moorhead, Linda, Scott, Clare and Gitters,
Howard (1999) 'Knowledge management, the new challenge for the 21st
century', *Journal of Knowledge Management*, 3(3): 172–9.

McDermott, Richard (1999) 'Why information technology inspired but
cannot deliver knowledge management', *California Management Review*,
41(4, Summer): 103–17.

McElroy, Mark W. (2000) 'Integrating complexity theory, knowledge
management and organizational learning', *Journal of Knowledge Management*, 3: 195–203.

Meso, Peter and Smith, Robert (2000) 'Resource based view of
organisational management systems', *Journal of Knowledge Management*,
4(3): 224–34.

Olin, Jack G., Greis, Noel P. and Kasarda, John D. (1999) 'Knowledge
management across multitier enterprises: the purposes of intelligent
software in the auto industry', *European Management Journal*, 17(4, Aug.):
335–47.

Pearce, Mark (1999) 'Knowledge management and the company secretary',
Chartered Secretary, Feb.: 24–5.

Perez-Bustamante, Guillermo (1999) 'Knowledge management in agile
innovative organisations', *Journal of Knowledge Management*, 3(1): 6–17.

Pfeffer, Jeffrey and Sutton, Robert (1999) *The Knowing Doing Gap: How
Smart Companies Turn Knowledge into Action*, Boston, MA: Harvard
Business School Press.

Pfeffer, Jeffrey and Sutton, Robert I. (1999) 'Knowing what to do is not enough: turning knowledge into action', *California Management Review*, 42(1, Fall): 83–108.

Probst, Gilbert, Raub, Steffen and Romhardy, Kai (2000) *Managing Knowledge: Building Blocks for Success*, Chichester: Wiley.

Rajan, Amin, Lank, Elisabeth and Chapple, Kirsty (1999) *Good Practices in Knowledge Creation and Exchange*, Tunbridge Wells: Centre for Research in Employment and Technology in Europe.

Rock, Stuart (ed.) (2000) *Business Guide to Liberating Knowledge*, London: Caspian.

Rock, Stuart (ed.) (1998) *Knowledge Management: a Real Business Guide*, London: Caspian.

Rossett, Allison (1999) 'Knowledge management meets analysis', *Training and Development USA*, 53(5, May): 63–8.

Ruddy, Tom (2000) 'Taking knowledge from heads and putting it into hands', *Knowledge and Process Management*, 7(1): 37–40.

Sanderson, Stuart M., Nixon, Adrian W. and Aran, Alan J. (2000) 'Adding value to a company's selling activity through knowledge management: a case study', *International Journal of Technology Management*, 20(5–8): 742–51.

Scarborough, Harry and Carter, Chris (2000) *Investigating Knowledge Management*, London: Chartered Institute of Personnel and Development,

Scarborough, Harry, Swan, Jacky and Preston, John (1999) *Knowledge Management: a Literature Review*, London: IPD.

Shadbolt, Nigel and Milton, Nick (1999) 'From knowledge engineering to knowledge management', *British Journal of Management*, 10(4, Dec.): 309–22.

Sieloff, Charles G. (1999) 'If only HP knew what HP knows: the roots of knowledge management at Hewlett Packard', *Journal of Knowledge Management*, 3(1): 47–53.

Skyrme, David J. (1999) *Knowledge Networking: Creating the Collaborative Enterprise*, Oxford: Butterworth Heinemann.

Spinello, Richard A. (1998) 'The knowledge chain', *Business Horizons*, 41(6, Nov.–Dec.): 4–14.

Storey, John and Barnett, Elizabeth (2000) 'Knowledge management initiatives: learning from failure', *Journal of Knowledge Management*, 4(2): 145–56.

Suff, Paul (2000) *Knowledge Management*, London: Eclipse.

TFPL Library and Information Commission (1999) *Skills for Knowledge Management: Building a Knowledge Economy*, London: Library and Information Commission.

Tyler, Geoff (1999) 'Well what dya know', *Management Services*, 43(6, June): 28–31.

Uit Beijerse, Roelof P. (1999) 'Questions in knowledge management:

defining and conceptualising a phenomenon', *Journal of Knowledge Management*, 3(2): 94–109.

Van Buren, Mark E. (1999) 'A yardstick for knowledge management', *Training and Development USA*, 53(5, May): 71–5.

vit Beijerse, R.P. (2000) 'Knowledge management in small and medium sized companies: knowledge management for entrepreneurs', *Journal of Knowledge Management*, 4(2): 162–79.

Wah, Louisa (1999) 'Behind the buzz', *Management Review*, Apr.: 16–26.

Wah, Louisa (1999) 'Making knowledge stick', *Management Review*, May: 24–9.

Warner, Malcolm and Witzel, Morgen (1999) 'Knowledge and the general manager', *Financial Times Mastering Management Review*, 26 August: 38–41.

Webb, Sylvia P. (1998) *Knowledge Management, Lynchpin of Change: Some Practical Guidelines*, London: Aslib.

Whitehead, Mark (1999) 'Collection time', *People Management*, 5(21, 28 Oct.): 68–71.

Wiig, Karl M. (1998) 'Knowledge management: an introduction and perspective', *International Journal of Business Transformation*, 1(3, Jan.): 162–70.

Willard, Nick (1999) 'Knowledge management foundations for a secure structure', *Managing Information*, 6(5, Jun.): 45–9.

Wilson, Owen (1998) 'Knowledge management: putting a good idea to work', *Managing Information*, 5(2, Mar.): 31–3.

Zack, Michael H. (1999) 'Developing a knowledge strategy', *California Management Review*, 41(3, Spring): 125–45.

Zack, Michael H. (1999) 'Managing codified knowledge', *Sloan Management Review*, 40(4, Summer): 45–58.

Zack, Michael H. (ed.) (1999) Knowledge and Strategy, Boston, MA: Harvard Business School Press.

ageism issues 112–13
alliances 170–4, 195, 203, 211,
    259–60
anticipatory learning concepts
    197
authentication requirements
    228–33

Balanced Scorecard methods
    70–8
benchmarks 19, 137, 142–5,
    203, 210, 246, 259
best practices 5, 19, 137, 142–5,
    245–6, 259
blame cultures 100, 212
Boo.com 22, 30, 172
brain structures 114–16
brainstorming sessions 44,
    206–7, 256
brands 63, 64–6, 259
'bricks and mortar' businesses
    13, 22–5, 38, 53, 184–7,
    201, 210
Business Excellence Model
    72–8
business models 25–7, 35–8,
    35–60, 157–9, 197–8
business process re-engineering
    (BPR) 18–19, 110
business to business (B2B)
    22–3, 25–7, 195

call centres 57
capturing knowledge 7–10,
    129–74, 203, 256
changes 6–21, 35–46, 55, 62–8,
    142–5, 184–7, 193–215,
    256–60
'clicks and mortar' businesses
    13, 22–5, 31–3, 53, 79,
    184–7, 201, 210
coaches 211–15
codification strategies 188–92
collaborations 172–4, 195,
    214
combination modes 88, 200
commitment factors 98–108,
    118–20, 194, 214, 245–6

communication issues 90–4,
    100, 145–8, 152–6, 194,
    203, 253, 257–61
communities of practice
    concepts 103–4, 136
competitive advantages 1–14,
    25–30, 63–4, 92, 109,
    129–49, 258–9
complexity issues 14, 37, 182–3,
    191, 259
confidentiality requirements
    228–33
continuous improvements 99,
    139–42, 246
copyrights 63, 68, 218–19,
    224–5
costs 3, 7–8, 53, 71–2, 137–40,
    163, 171, 211, 259
creating knowledge 3, 7–16,
    26–7, 30–1, 86–97, 141–2,
    151–74, 175–92
creative destruction concepts
    213–15
cultures 1–10, 16, 46–8, 62–8,
    89–100, 142–5, 178–80,
    193–215, 256–72
customers 2–6, 32–3, 46–66,
    70–8, 145–8, 157–9,
    164–70, 200–1, 259–60
customisation concepts 47–8,
    156

data 8, 27, 164–5
decision making 37–9, 66,
    206
deregulations 43
design rights 218, 221–2
domain names 227–33

e-business 1–11, 62–4, 71–8,
    96–7, 187–92, 217–33,
    258–9
    see also Internet
    concepts 6–10, 62–4, 71–8,
    111–12, 151–74, 203–4,
    259–60
economic factors 42–6, 139,
    171–2

empowerment issues 9, 67–8,
    82, 97–102, 178, 194–5,
    214, 256
encryption issues 227–31
energy concepts 1–11, 258–9
entrepreneurial cultures 1, 6,
    62, 127, 159–61, 175–86
entry/exit barriers 28–9
environmental issues 6, 9–10,
    16, 35, 42–6, 62, 139, 203,
    259–60
equity theories 105
expectancy theory concepts
    105–8
experiential learning concepts
    199
explicit knowledge 2–3, 87–9,
    94
externalisation modes 88, 200
extranets 8, 10, 49, 68, 163, 256

feedback issues 33, 62, 65–6,
    91–2, 113, 210–11
financial perspectives, Balanced
    Scorecard perspectives
    70–8

generative learning concepts
    197–8
globalisation drivers 20–1, 43,
    62
goal setting theories 104–5
groups 87–9, 103–4, 134–9,
    206–7, 246, 258

Herzberg's dual factor theory
    102, 104–8

ideas 56, 177, 183–4, 224
imagination concepts 175
imitations 191
impact analysis concepts 43–6
incubator concepts 178–82
industrial property concepts
    218–19
information 8, 16, 17–19,
    27–33, 164–5, 175

information technology (IT)
18–19, 224, 227–33
innovations 2–4, 11, 28, 52–3,
66–82, 99, 156, 169,
175–92, 214, 259–61
instrumentality concepts 106
intangible assets 2–17, 56–84,
109, 259–60
integrity requirements 228–33
intellectual capital 8–9, 16, 27,
32, 56, 63–8, 80–2, 194,
224–5
intellectual property issues,
legal dimensions 217–33
intelligence concepts 175
internalisation modes 88–9, 200
Internet 113–14, 152–4, 163–8,
187–92, 256
see also e-business
concepts 6–10, 21–2, 62–4,
93–4, 151–74, 256–61
legal issues 191, 227–33
intranets 8, 10, 49, 68, 138,
163–5, 246, 256, 260
inventions 176–7, 218, 220–1

judgements 38, 41

knowledge 175–92, 199–215,
256–9
concepts 2–11, 19–33, 55–60,
86–7, 129–49, 255–72
definitions 27–31
information contrasts 8,
17–19, 27–31, 175
maps 129–49, 189–90, 246,
256
power 101–2, 132, 256
tacit knowledge 2–3, 82,
86–9, 94, 109, 116–17,
190–2, 199–201, 256
knowledge management 163–8,
256
concepts 2–11, 19–33,
85–108, 163–8, 235–6,
255–72
cynicism problems 17–18
definitions 16

leadership issues 6, 72–8, 90,
97, 119, 186, 193, 211–15,
256–72, 260–72
learning organisations 10, 16,
142–5, 193–215, 256–9
learning perspectives 70–8,
193–215
legal issues 191, 217–33
leverage issues 5–6, 8–10, 16,
18, 36–7, 56, 64, 67–8, 194,
245–6, 253
⁓s 169–70, 201, 259

maintenance learning concepts
196–7
management issues 67–82, 186,
193, 210–15, 232, 256–72
maps 129–49, 189–90, 246, 256
Maslow's hierarchy of needs
102–4
mental model disciplines
205–15, 257
mentors 211–15
motivation issues 99, 102–8,
120, 201–2, 256
multiple futures see scenario
planning

new economy drivers 9, 15–16,
20–33, 48–51, 119, 137–8,
172, 203–4, 210–15
North Atlantic Free Trade
Association (NAFTA) 20

organisations 31–3, 131,
138–41, 175–92, 261–72
outsourcing concepts 52–6,
188–9

partnerships 1, 7, 36, 50, 55,
170–4, 189, 195, 203, 211,
259–60
patents 63, 68, 78, 218–19,
220–1
perceptions 41
performance issues 5, 14–19,
32, 63–84, 137, 140–5, 203,
210, 245–6, 258–60, 270–2
personalisation strategies
189–92
plans 35–46, 140–3
political factors 20–1, 42–6, 139
power, knowledge 101–2, 132,
256
predictions 40–1
privatisations 43
product life cycles 52–3
profits 5, 7–8, 53, 70–2, 259–60

quality requirements 64–8,
72–8, 99, 133, 139–48, 238,
246
questionnaire 261–72

recruitment issues 53, 109–28,
178, 259–60
research and development
(R&D) 15, 56, 172, 178–80
retention issues 116–28, 178,
201, 259
revenues 5, 7–8, 53, 71–2, 171,
226, 247–53, 259–60
risks 3, 37–46, 201–2, 210–15,
232, 259

satisficing concepts 30
scenario planning 35, 39–46
security issues 227–33
seven S framework 186–7,
260–1
shared knowledge concepts
3–6, 32, 82, 86–108,
129–92, 211, 256–61
Silicon Valley 181, 185–6, 206
single-loop learning concepts
197–8
skills 90–4, 100, 110–11,
129–49, 171–2, 174, 186–7,
195, 256–7, 260
socialisation modes 87–8,
199–200
sociological factors 42–6, 139
STEP factors 42–6, 139
strategies 9, 14–33, 35–84, 119,
170–4, 186–95, 210–11,
232, 259–60
stretch concepts 7, 71, 183
structures 11, 78–82, 114–16,
186, 260
suppliers 7, 9–10, 25–7, 29,
50–2, 157–9
SWOT analysis 138–42
systems 186–92, 207–9, 256,
258–9, 260

tacit knowledge concepts 2–3,
82, 86–9, 94, 109, 116–17,
190–2, 199–201, 256
tangible assets 62–3, 70
teams 87–9, 103–4, 134–9,
206–15, 246, 258
technological factors 42–6,
68–9, 82, 139
total quality management
(TQM) 67–8, 72–8, 238,
246
trade secrets 222–3
trademarks 218, 223–4, 227–33
training 4, 89–92, 100, 247–53,
257
transferring knowledge 3–10,
58, 82–108, 141–2, 151–92,
211, 256
trust 5, 67–8, 89–102, 107, 132,
169–73, 178, 205–6,
228–33

valence concepts 106–8
value chains 7, 22–7, 46–52,
68–9, 157–9, 171, 200–1,
259
vision 6, 10, 62, 119, 194,
206–15, 258